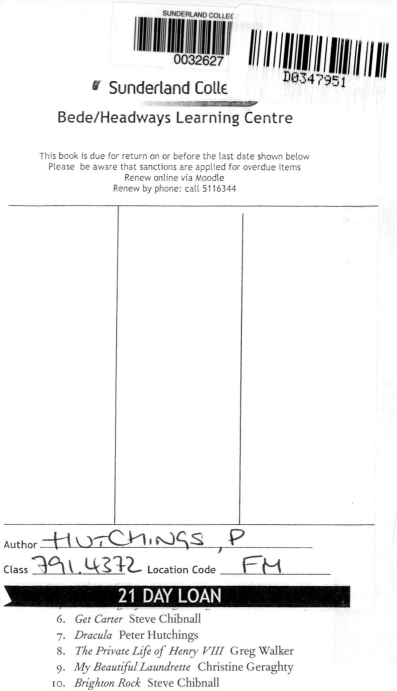

6. *Get Carter* Steve Chibnall
7. *Dracula* Peter Hutchings
8. *The Private Life of Henry VIII* Greg Walker
9. *My Beautiful Laundrette* Christine Geraghty
10. *Brighton Rock* Steve Chibnall
11. *The Red Shoes* Mark Connelly

THE BRITISH FILM GUIDE 7

Dracula

PETER HUTCHINGS

I.B. TAURIS

LONDON · NEW YORK

Published in 2003 by I.B.Tauris & Co. Ltd
6 Salem Road, London w2 4BU
175 Fifth Avenue, New York NY 10010
www.ibtauris.com

In the United States of America and Canada distributed by Palgrave
Macmillan, a division of St Martin's Press, 175 Fifth Avenue, New York
NY 10010

ISBN 1 86064 748 0

A full CIP record for this book is available from the British Library
A full CIP record for this book is available from the Library of Congress

Library of Congress catalog card: available

Set in Monotype Fournier and Univers Black by Ewan Smith, London
Printed and bound in Great Britain by MPG Books, Bodmin

Contents

Illustrations

The illustrations are from the author's collection, apart from numbers 8 and 9 which are reproduced by courtesy of the Ronald Grant Archive.

Film Credits

DRACULA 1958 (US: *THE HORROR OF DRACULA*)

Production Company	Hammer
Studio	Bray
Executive Producer	Michael Carreras
Producer	Anthony Hinds
Associate Producer	Anthony Nelson Keys
Director	Terence Fisher
Screenplay	Jimmy Sangster, based on the novel by Bram Stoker
Photography	Jack Asher
Supervising Editor	James Needs
Production Designer	Bernard Robinson
Music	James Bernard
Conductor	John Hollingsworth
Sound Recordist	Jock May
Editor	Bill Lenny
Production Manager	Don Weeks
Assistant Director	Bob Lynn
Camera Operator	Len Harris
Makeup	Philip Leakey
Hair Stylist	Henry Montsash
Continuity	Doreen Dearnaley
Wardrobe	Molly Arbuthnot
Special Effects	Sydney Pearson (and an uncredited Les Bowie)
Running Time	82 minutes
UK Première	22 May 1958
US Première	28 May 1958

CAST

Peter Cushing	Dr Van Helsing
Christopher Lee	Dracula
Michael Gough	Arthur Holmwood
Melissa Stribling	Mina Holmwood
Carol Marsh	Lucy Holmwood

Olga Dickie	Gerda
John Van Eyssen	Jonathan Harker
Valerie Gaunt	Vampire Woman
Janine Faye	Tania, Gerda's daughter
Barbara Archer	Inga
Charles Lloyd Pack	Dr Seward
George Merritt	Policeman
George Woodbridge	Landlord
George Benson	Official
Miles Malleson	Undertaker
Geoffrey Bayldon	Porter
Paul Cole	Lad

The following actors are included in some reference sources but do not actually appear in the film.

Stedwell Fulcher	Man in Coach
Humphrey Kent	Fat Merchant
Guy Mills	Coach Driver
Dick Morgan	Coach Driver's Companion
Judith Nelmes	Woman in Coach
William Sherwood	Priest

Introduction

There has been a tendency in some recent writing on British cinema to shy away from making evaluative judgements. Films are seen as 'interesting' rather than as 'good films' (or 'bad films'). This reluctance to assign value can perhaps be related to the greater awareness we have today of the relative and contingent nature of value judgements and the ways in which these express and depend on class and gender-based ideologies. From such a perspective, evaluative readings have the potential to undermine any approach concerned to establish what a film's significance might be. From another perspective, however, this is all to the good for the undermining of interpretative authority opens up the interpretation itself to critical scrutiny.

In the interests of clarity and openness, then, I need to make explicit from the beginning a judgement that will permeate this whole book, namely that, in my view, the Hammer *Dracula* of 1958 is not just an interesting film but also a remarkably good film. A considerable part of this book will be devoted to an exploration of the reasons why I think this, primarily through a detailed discussion of *Dracula* itself. To a certain extent, this sort of approach – one that involves working methodically through a particular film – has fallen out of favour in the study of British cinema, largely, one suspects, because of the association of evaluative textual analysis with an auteur-based understanding of film. Auteurism's concern to identify the auteur-director's personal signature within a film's *mise-en-scène* has, since the late 1960s, come to be seen as obscuring the collaborative and industrial nature of film production. Recent work on audiences has also encouraged us to see meaning residing not in the details of a film itself but instead in the ways in which that film has been received by particular audiences. Meaning becomes here part of a social and historical process rather than something that is textually fixed.

There are good reasons, then, for turning away from the close textual analysis of films, and our understanding of British cinema has undoubtedly benefited from the work that has been done on the industry and the audiences for British films. However, there is still something to be said for looking at (and evaluating) individual films in detail. This is partly because films themselves are not wholly defined by the various contexts of their reception; they are also objects that are moulded by the context of their production. Over-emphasising the importance of an audience's perception of cinema can make it difficult to grasp why films actually get made in the way that they do. The other reason for focusing on an individual film is, of course, an evaluative one, and it involves identifying how the film in question deploys the resources of cinema in an imaginative, intelligent and distinctive manner.

Such an approach does not have to be an auteur-based one. While auteurist claims have been made for Terence Fisher, the director of the Hammer *Dracula*, the account this book will offer of *Dracula* will not prioritise his input but will instead seek to relate it to the input of the other key creative personnel involved in the film's production. Neither will my account of the film be ahistorical; on the contrary, I do not believe that the distinctiveness of *Dracula* is comprehensible without reference to the circumstances of the film's production and its position within both the history of British cinema and the history of the horror genre. I will also discuss the ways in which *Dracula* has been interpreted and reinterpeted in the years since its production, suggesting some of the reasons for changes in its critical fortunes.

At the same time, the book will consider *Dracula* as an artefact that, while formed within a particular context and subsequently passing through other contexts, has maintained a distinctive specificity of its own. The book will not be concerned to establish what *Dracula* 'really' means; as already noted, meaning tends to be context-specific (and where I do discuss meaning, I will seek to explain the context within which my own interpretation is operating). But a detailed attention to a film's structure, the techniques it deploys, and its *mise-en-scène*, can produce a clearer sense of the film itself as an object.

It seems to me that this kind of approach is indispensable to any evaluative claims for British cinema (and, despite all the new work being done on British film, evaluative claims are not being made nearly enough). It is also an approach that can provide a positive contribution to the historical methodologies that have helped to form the study of British cinema over the past two decades. Too often some of this historical work has contained implicit, unspoken value judgements about what makes a film interesting or good. It is surely better to bring these judgements out into the open, to make them explicit and discuss them.

Accordingly, this book will seek to combine a contextual analysis of *Dracula*'s production and critical reception with an evaluation of the film as an aesthetic object. Not only do we need to understand the historical and cultural significance of the Hammer *Dracula*; we also need to think about what it is that makes this *Dracula* a good film.

ONE
Dracula Lives!

THE COMING ATTRACTION

Imagine that you are walking down a British city street during the summer of 1958. Ahead is a poster advertising the release of a new film. Against a black background, a man leans over a woman, his hand resting on her shoulder. From a distance, and if you are not paying much attention, it could be mistaken for a romantic pose. Move closer, however, and things start to change. You can see the man's face more clearly now; his features are contorted into a snarl and his firm grasp on the woman suggests an act of violent possessiveness. The woman herself seems oblivious to the man's presence. Her eyes are closed. Is she asleep, unconscious, or perhaps even dead? More details appear. You see that the man's canine teeth are elongated and sharp. And then you notice that there is a suggestion of a smile on the woman's face. It is as if she is anticipating some pleasurable event while, perplexingly, the rest of the image speaks of a violent assault.

Move your eyes to the left now, and the enigma of this image immediately becomes somewhat less enigmatic. DRACULA. The word lacks an exclamation mark, but the boldness of the typeface, the size of the letters, and the fact that they are coloured a garish red underline not only their importance but also their potency. In the top left of the poster you then see 'The Terrifying Lover – Who Died – Yet Lived!' (with an exclamation mark this time) and in the bottom right corner 'DON'T DARE SEE IT ALONE!' (with another exclamation mark). You relax. Just another *Dracula* movie.

In certain respects this encounter with the poster for the first *Dracula* film to be produced by the Hammer company is an unlikely one. Not that the poster was not being displayed in Britain in 1958; rather that the picture sketched here of a casual passer-by ineluctably drawn into a contemplation of a mysterious image depends on that passer-by failing to notice from the word go the large red DRACULA that cuts across the middle of the poster. However, there is something to be said for the idea that this poster, like many film posters, operates on two levels. One of these concerns itself with offering something familiar, while the other offers something new. The familiar – for that 1958 pedestrian – is likely to have been the word DRACULA itself, familiar not only from Bram Stoker's original 1897 novel but also, and possibly to a greater degree, from the various stage and film adaptations that had appeared from the 1920s onwards. In fact, the most famous film version of *Dracula* at that time – the 1931 Universal production starring Bela Lugosi as Count Dracula – had been playing in London and elsewhere in the country (on a double bill with the 1931 version of *Frankenstein*) as recently as 1955.[1] For the passer-by with a long memory, the slogan 'The Terrifying Lover – Who Died – Yet Lived!' – along with another slogan used in the film's marketing, 'Who Will Be His Bride Tonight?' – would also have been more than a little reminiscent of the slogan with which the 1931 *Dracula* had been launched: 'The story of the strangest passion the world has ever known'.[2]

Hammer's poster offered something new as well. The fangs, for example. Lugosi had not worn fangs; nor had any of his vampiric successors such as Lon Chaney Junior (Dracula in *The Son of Dracula*, 1943), John Carradine (Dracula in *House of Frankenstein*, 1944 and *House of Dracula*, 1945), and Francis Lederer (in *The Return of Dracula*, 1958). To find a befanged vampire, you would have had to track down a critically acclaimed but hard-to-see German film from 1922, F. W. Murnau's *Nosferatu: A Symphony of Terror*, and even there the fangs were different, rodent-like incisors rather than the more dignified canine fangs sported by the Hammer Dracula. And who is this Dracula? The poster credits the role to Christopher Lee, but who is he? A film-goer from 1958 might well remember the name from the Hammer horror film that had appeared the previous year, *The Curse of Frankenstein*, where Lee, heavily made-up and barely recognisable as the same man featured on the *Dracula* poster, had played Frankenstein's Creature. A particularly observant film-goer might even have recalled seeing Lee before in small parts in over thirty British films from the late 1940s onwards. But to all intents and purposes, the face of Dracula that appears on Hammer's poster is new to British cinema. A new *Dracula* film, then, with a new-look Dracula, and, as the poster informs us by announcing that the film is 'In Eastman Colour processed by Technicolor', the first *Dracula* film (and, in fact, the first vampire film) to be in colour.

In other ways, too, the poster's picturing of Dracula and his female victim suggests a revised take on the vampire story. There is a physicality to the image, with Dracula's hand powerfully grasping the woman's shoulder (and resting very near her left breast) which was uncommon in previous *Dracula* films where the physical business of blood-letting occurred offscreen and where onscreen the Count usually contented himself with giving people a nasty stare. This physicality is underlined by a certain aggression apparent in the image's composition – not only is Dracula leaning out towards us but the woman also seems to be almost falling out of the poster. It is as if the poster itself can barely contain these two figures. (This feature was even more pronounced on the marquee display outside the Gaumont Haymarket Cinema in London's West End where the film first opened in May 1958. Here the victim's long hair appears to be falling down the front of the cinema itself.)

From our present-day perspective, of course, the 'shock value' of the Hammer poster has been largely, if not completely, dissipated, to the extent that there is now a faintly nostalgic tinge to this image of Dracula. We know now who Christopher Lee is and what he looks like. Vampires in colour – so what? Vampires with fangs – what else do you expect? And, in the age of *Buffy the Vampire Slayer* and *Angel*, we confidently expect our vampires to be physically powerful. It follows that in order to reclaim the 'shock value', to grasp what is distinctive both about the poster and the film that it advertises, we have to think ourselves back into the mind of our fictional pedestrian as he strolls past the poster in 1958. As should now be clear, this might be a casual encounter but it is also a historically specific one; it relates to and itself is part of what might be termed here a history of *Dracula* (or, to be more precise, a history of Draculas). As we will see, it is a history that is far from straightforward and which contains more than a few surprises.

What follows in this chapter is an account of the pre-history of the Hammer *Dracula*. It tells how a story that first appeared in literary form in Britain in 1897 made its away across decades and continents before ending up back in Britain sixty-one years later. It also explains why it was that the national cinema of the country in which the original novel was written (albeit by an Irish novelist) did not get round to making a film of it until 1958. However, before embarking on this exploration of *Dracula*'s development over the years and the various contexts of that development, it is necessary to consider some of the broader claims that have been made for the *Dracula* story as a myth of some kind, either as a late-Victorian myth that has somehow survived into our present or as a modern myth still relevant to our lives. In part, this is useful because so many of the critical and journalistic writings on *Dracula* address it in mythic terms. But for the purposes of this book, which focuses on one particular version of *Dracula*, it is also necessary to think about the relation between the story's mythic status – which implies a certain timelessness – and the way in which the story is constantly being reworked in order to make it relevant to and timely for particular markets. In other words, we need to consider the relation between the idea of *Dracula* as cultural myth or archetype and *Dracula* as a piece of popular/exploitation fiction.

THE SECRET LIFE OF *DRACULA*

A survey of the critical writings on Bram Stoker's 1897 novel *Dracula* reveals an array of approaches and attitudes. One thing underpins them all, however. This is the sense that, so far as *Dracula* is concerned, nothing is what it seems, and that in order to grasp the true significance of the novel one has to go beneath its surface, passing through its literal meanings in order to discover a series of hidden scandalous secrets. Seen in this way, *Dracula* is not (as one critic has put it) 'a spoiled masterpiece', but instead a masterpiece of the unconscious, the symptomatic, the unintended, a work which seems to operate independently of the conscious intent of its author, and the significance of which was barely recognised on the book's first appearance in the late-Victorian period.[3]

This very pervasive way of thinking about the novel is greatly aided by what might be termed Bram Stoker's non-canonical position within British literature. To put it bluntly, he is no George Eliot or Charles Dickens; he is not even a Wilkie Collins (although, in structural terms at least, *Dracula* owes something to Collins's novel *The Woman in White*). It is hard to find any critic who is willing to make a wholehearted case for Stoker as a 'great' or even 'good' writer in the conventional sense of those terms. A few valiantly make an attempt but seem to give up almost immediately. For example, literary historian David Punter describes *Dracula* as a 'well-written and formally inventive sensation novel' but then adds that the novel's significance has less to do with Stoker's own perceptions and more with the way it functions, presumably unconsciously, 'as a powerful record of social pressures and anxieties';[4] while horror historian David J. Skal, in the context of a favourable discussion of *Dracula*'s cultural significance, compares Stoker's novel

1. *The poster for the British release of* Dracula.

unfavourably with Mary Shelley's *Frankenstein* so far as literary value is concerned: 'Where *Frankenstein* is literary and philosophical, *Dracula* is a naïve entertainment engaging the emotions rather than the intellect.'[5]

One can claim that Stoker's lowly cultural status has more to do with the type of Gothic fiction he was writing. Certainly some of the qualities of *Dracula* which offended and continue to offend some critics – its sprawling structure, its moralistic tone, its graceless and overly rhetorical style, its schematic characterisations – are actually more general features of the Gothic form and are readily apparent in earlier 'classic' Gothics such as Ann Radcliffe's *The Mysteries of Udolpho* (1794) and *The Italian* (1797), Matthew 'Monk' Lewis's *The Monk* (1796), Mary Shelley's *Frankenstein* (1818) and Charles Maturin's *Melmoth, the Wanderer* (1820). Some literary historians have argued that the value of this type of Gothic fiction lies precisely in the challenge it offers to conventional literary standards that are often based on notions of realism and restraint. In its systematic fracturing of notions of identity and in its focusing on intense psychological states, the Gothic novel presents a potentially very modern take on the human condition in a bourgeois, capitalist world. As Rosemary Jackson, author of a key text on Gothic and fantasy fiction, puts it: 'The subject is no longer confident about appropriating or perceiving a material world. Gothic narrates this epistemological confusion: it expresses and examines personal disorder, opposing fiction's classical unities (of time, space, unified character) with an apprehension of partiality and relativity of meaning.'[6]

Whether or not one agrees with this as a reading of Gothic fiction in general, it does seem that even those critics interested in pursuing the Gothic as a kind of oppositional form often balk at seeing *Dracula* in these terms. This might have something to do with the fact that *Dracula* comes along much later than the original Gothics and that it does not offer itself up for literary analysis in the way that those earlier novels do. Or perhaps some of the novel's ostensible values, which to a present-day eye can seem remarkably reactionary, get in the way of thinking of it as any kind of critique; certainly the novel is regularly accused of being sexist and racist. Or perhaps it is just the relentless popularity of the novel – never out of print since 1897 – and the dispersal of the *Dracula* narrative across film, television and theatre that discourages critics from considering the original text as in itself significant. Whatever the reason, *Dracula*'s position within literary work on the Gothic tends to be a marginal one.

A further diminution in Stoker's authorial status arguably derives from the fact that, so far as his position in literary history is concerned, he has come to be seen as a one-book author. Some of his short stories – notably 'The Judge's House' and 'The Squaw' (the latter a particularly nasty horror tale), along with a chapter originally discarded from *Dracula* and later published as 'Dracula's Guest' – have been regularly antholo-gised, and his supernatural novels *The Jewel of the Seven Stars* (1903) and *The Lair of the White Worm* (1911) have minor cult followings. However, the prolific Stoker's other publications – which include the novels *The Snake's Pass* (1890), *The Mystery of the Sea* (1902), *The Man* (1905) and *Lady Athlyne* (1908) as well as factual works such as *Personal Reminiscences of Henry Irving* (1906) and *Famous Imposters* (1910) – are much less well-known than *Dracula*. In fact, such is the disparity between the obscurity of most of Stoker's work and the distinctiveness of *Dracula* that it has led some to speculate that other writers must have had a hand in the novel's creation (although the biographical evidence indicating that Stoker worked on *Dracula* for a much longer period than on any of his other books suggests another reason, albeit a less exciting and dram-atic one, for its superiority).[7]

If not as an expression of a substantial authorial presence, then where

do the significance and meaning of *Dracula* lie? *Dracula* criticism offers
two distinct (although sometimes related) responses to this. One, which
might reasonably be termed the 'historicist' approach, seeks to locate
the novel firmly within the socio-historical context of its creation and
initial reception. The novel is seen as crystallising and attempting to
manage and contain all manner of fears and anxieties pertaining to
Britain in the late-Victorian period – notably fears to do with a perceived
decline in the British Empire and an accompanying racial degeneration,
and anxieties caused by the changing role of women as manifested in
particular in debates about 'the New Woman'. In doing this, the novel
deploys a range of historically specific discourses – about gender and
sexuality, about race, about national identity – that are circulating more
widely in Victorian society and Victorian culture, and which are not
necessarily used in the novel in either a self-conscious or a cohesive
manner. Depending on how one values the novel, *Dracula* emerges from
this either as something of a mess, albeit one that is inadvertently
revealing about certain aspects of Victorian life, or as a 'dialogical'
novel, a work which juxtaposes different narrators and different discourses in a manner that, potentially and perhaps also inadvertently,
critiques 'the conditions, processes, and motivations upon which the
production, circulation, and exchange of its discourses depend'.[8] In
either case, Stoker's authorship does not count for much; he becomes
merely the vehicle through which either broader social attitudes or a
literary/generic self-reflexivity are manifested. So, for example, art
historian Bram Dijkstra relates the roles of the woman in *Dracula* to a
broader continuum of late-Victorian representations of the sexualised
woman, literary scholars Stephen D. Arata and David Punter locate the
novel in relation to other Victorian texts dealing with anxieties about
racial degeneracy, while Marxist theorist Franco Moretti discusses *Dracula* as a representation of fears about Britain's economic status.[9]

It is fair to say that this sort of approach, less respectful than before
of the authority of the author or the necessary cohesiveness of his/her
work and more interested in the context within which the work was
produced and received, is becoming increasingly important and pervasive in literary criticism. It is also fair to say that it is probably easier
to do this with a non-canonical novelist like Stoker for his marginality
in traditional literary hierarchies means that he has accrued less respect
as a literary figure than canonical figures such as Jane Austen or George
Eliot. This is probably why stage and film adaptations of *Dracula* have
rarely been criticised for deviating from the original novel (although

they all do, often to a very great extent indeed), while adaptations of more highly valued novels are even now scrutinised much more closely on this account. (One thinks here of a recent film version of Jane Austen's *Mansfield Park* which had the temerity to include lesbian elements and references to the slave trade and which was roundly criticised for not being respectful of the original.) It is interesting in this light that a recent study of Bram Stoker – David Glover's *Vampires, Mummies and Liberals: Bram Stoker and the Politics of Popular Fiction* – not only seems firmly wedded to this symptomatic approach but also uses it as a way of finding value in literary work. Glover argues not that Stoker is a 'great' author in a traditional sense but rather that 'Stoker's lapses and inconsistencies are what make his writing so compelling, for they show his novels and stories to be the work of a transitional figure, an author nervously glancing back at the past as he strides out into the future.'[10]

Seen in this way, Count Dracula himself becomes, in one critic's words, 'the supreme bogeyman – a creature who means different things to different people'.[11] An amorphous figure, the threat he presents can at one moment be intensely erotic, and at another moment be primarily racial, the threat of the foreigner to English national identity. It is almost as if the lack of authority imputed to Stoker as author by critics is reflected in the novel's failure to pin down Dracula in any singular form or meaning.

This historicist work on *Dracula* has proved very valuable in opening up the novel to critical and historical scrutiny. However, it is probably of limited value when one is seeking to explain the persistence of *Dracula* in our culture since the novel's original publication. Presumably the socially specific anxieties that occupied the Victorians, and to which *Dracula* itself was a kind of response, are either not operative for us or exist in very different forms. So, for example, when Bram Dijkstra seeks to establish a continuity between the novel's original historical context and the present by claiming that contemporary vampire fictions 'are still unconsciously responding very directly to an antifeminine sensibility established in its modern form and symbolic structure by the sexist ideologues among the nineteenth-century intelligentsia', he has to rely on historical generalities that sit uneasily with the more specific and detailed account of a particular moment in late-Victorian culture he offers elsewhere.[12]

If historicist accounts comprise one way of thinking about *Dracula*, Dijkstra's passing reference above to the unconscious appeal of the vampire points to the other important approach to Stoker's creation –

one that is based firmly on the tenets of psychoanalysis. The stress here, as it usually is in psychoanalysis, is on the sexual, on the erotic threat posed by the vampire and the 'monstrous' desires he invokes in others, particularly his female victims. Here the novel tends to be seen as emerging from, and giving us access to, the unconscious, be this Stoker's unconscious, a Victorian collective unconscious, or the unconscious in general.

As some critics have noted, there is nothing inherently ahistorical about psychoanalysis, but in practice psychoanalytical approaches to culture often have an ahistorical or universalising dimension. Psycho-analytical accounts of *Dracula* are no exception to this. While they frequently deploy contextualising elements, often to do with Victorian sexual mores, the emphasis on sexuality as a force that in some way exists outside of history undermines any claims they might have to be historical in any systematic or comprehensive way. Psychoanalytical approaches tend to posit *Dracula* as an erotically transgressive text, one that offers a challenge to conventional Victorian notions – and perhaps also more contemporary notions – of normative sexuality. As David Pirie puts it: 'On one level at least, the character of the Count can be construed as the great submerged force of Victorian libido breaking out to punish the repressive society which had imprisoned it.'[13]

Seen from this perspective, Stoker himself becomes a more interesting figure, not as the controlling author but rather as the unwitting, un-knowing source of this eroticism, that for which the novel itself is an eloquent symptom. Ironically perhaps, Stoker's own somewhat enigmatic persona does not help much in this respect. His life story – which takes in a movement from being a civil servant in Dublin to working in London for Henry Irving, one of the leading actors of his day (and, according to some, the model for Dracula himself) – appears to have been surprisingly undramatic. However, this lack of dramatic incident and conflict has not stopped some biographers from offering largely speculative accounts of Stoker's sexuality and sexual behaviour. For example, Daniel Farson (who was Stoker's grand-nephew) has claimed that Stoker frequented prostitutes and died of syphilis (a claim disputed by other biographers), while others – on the basis of little more than some fan letters sent by Stoker to American poet Walt Whitman, his devotion to Henry Irving, and his distant connection with Oscar Wilde (he married a woman previously admired by Wilde) – have asserted that the author of *Dracula* was either gay or bisexual.[14] The assumption behind this rather fevered speculation appears to derive directly from a reading of Stoker's work. How, these biographers ask, can the author of a novel as sexually perverse as *Dracula*, and the possessor of a literary imagination that was 'a bleeding bottomless pit of bisexual ambivalence', possibly be straight?[15]

Other psychoanalytical accounts have shown less interest in exploring Stoker's psychology and have focused instead on the appeal of the vampire myth itself. Of key significance here is Ernest Jones's book *On the Nightmare* (1931) which does not discuss *Dracula* at all but which does offer a provocative and influential reading of what Jones sees as the essentially sexual nature of the vampire. Jones was one of the first to make what has now become – in critical writing at least – a fairly commonplace association between blood and semen:

> A nightly visit from a beautiful or frightful being, who first exhausts the sleeper with passionate embraces and then withdraws from him a vital fluid: all this can point only to a natural and common process, namely to nocturnal emissions accompanied with dreams of a more or less erotic nature. In the unconscious mind blood is commonly an equivalent for semen.[16]

The fact that Jones is clearly referring here to a male victim rather than the more usual female victim associated with *Dracula* has not stopped later critics from using his work as the basis for their own increasingly complex readings of Stoker's novel and various adaptations of it.

Notable in this respect is Maurice Richardson who in an article from 1959, entitled 'The Psychoanalysis of Ghost Stories', argues that Sigmund Freud's book *Totem and Taboo* can help us understand what *Dracula* is really about. In the bizarre quasi-anthropological scenario offered by *Totem and Taboo*, a group of young men, jealous of a greedy father who keeps all the women to himself, band together to kill and consume the father and then erect a totem to his memory. Richardson suggests that in *Dracula* the Count himself is the monstrous father while the young men of the novel – namely Arthur Godalming, Jonathan Harker, John Seward and Quincey Morris – comprise the 'primal horde' described by Freud in *Totem and Taboo*, helped in this case by a good father figure in the shape of Abraham van Helsing. The resulting narrative 'turns out to be a quite blatant demonstration of the Oedipus complex ... a kind of incestuous, necrophilous, oral-anal-sadistic, all-in-wrestling match'.[17]

Other critics have explored what they see as the novel's pre-Oedipal dimension and its apparent concern with 'the child's relation with and hostility toward the mother',[18] with the mother covertly or symbolically represented by female 'victims' Lucy and Mina. In a phrase that will make all but the most die-hard follower of psychoanalysis wince, Roger Dadoun has gone so far as to describe the Count himself as a 'substitute for the mother's penis'.[19] By contrast, a more restrained Christopher Craft has argued that the novel contains distinct homoerotic elements as well as a representation of a broader instability in gender definition.[20]

Amidst the various polymorphous perversities conjured up by the psychoanalytical critics, James B. Twitchell provides a rare straight-forwardly heterosexual account of the vampire myth in his book *Dreadful Pleasures: An Anatomy of Modern Horror*. The stress on the sexual nature of the vampire remains but, for Twitchell, 'horror sequences are really formulaic rituals coded with precise social information needed by the adolescent audience'.[21] He might have added that for him this 'precise social information' relates in an unproblematic and unequivocal way to how to be a heterosexual with, in the case of the vampire narrative, the male adolescents in the audience identifying with the male vampire and female adolescents identifying with the female victim. The possibility of something as perverse as cross-gender identification and an attendant disruption of sexual norms is clearly not on Twitchell's agenda. What he does share with other psychoanalytical critics (and to a certain extent with the historicist critics as well) is a sense of the artlessness of the novel *Dracula* ('If *Dracula*'s claim on our attention is not artistic, it must be psychological')[22] which he extends to 'the unaffected and artless return of the vampire back into popular culture'.[23]

It is clear from Twitchell's work in particular that the psychoanalytical approach to *Dracula* does potentially offer an account not only of the original novel but also the various stage and film adaptations that followed. Inasmuch as these adaptations are plugged into notions of the Oedipal and the pre-Oedipal – concepts often seen as transhistorical – their recurrence in our culture speaks of an ongoing, ceaseless confrontation with deep-seated and immutable psychological fears and anxieties. However, there are some rather obvious problems associated both with this way of thinking about *Dracula* and with the psychoanalytical approach to culture in general. The privileging of the sexual over issues to do with racial and class difference arguably neglects key elements in the *Dracula* story – namely the vampire's foreignness and his aristocracy. The draining away of any sense of historical context certainly permits a forging of connections between the various stage and film versions of *Dracula* that appeared from the 1920s onwards but only at the expense of reducing these to an expression of some singular, essential meaning and function. This is most explicit in Twitchell's account of the vampire where he indicates that his emphasis will not be on 'artful' vampire films, films which might deviate from that core meaning, but instead on the 'artless' products of popular culture (which, for Twitchell, include Hammer's 1958 version of *Dracula*), texts which because of their lack of self-awareness offer a clearer picture of horror's instructive function.

Such an approach makes it difficult to identify that which is distinctive about Hammer's *Dracula*. Is this film really just another 'unconscious' or unwitting expression of some psychosexual complex deeply embedded in our culture? Are its differences from other *Dracula* adaptations – precisely those elements that, as we have seen, sustain the poster's shock value – insignificant window-dressing for what is essentially just another retelling of the same old story?

To a certain extent, such questions are imponderable ones. Saying that an individual has an unconscious is one thing; imputing an unconscious of some kind either to culture or to society itself is something else entirely, something more contentious, more provocative. One wonders in this respect how it was that when Stoker's novel was originally published, no one seemed to notice the various sexual perversities that the psychoanalytical method has since discovered. One possible answer, the psychoanalytical answer, is that the purpose of psychoanalysis is precisely to reveal that which was originally hidden or repressed; i.e. the late-Victorian audience did not really understand the novel but we can understand it now. However, another answer might be that the psychoanalytical discourses deployed by various critics have encouraged them to see the novel primarily in erotic terms while late-Victorian readers, and perhaps later audiences as well, might simply have been making sense of the vampire in different ways, ways more relevant to their own historical situation. Literary historian David Glover puts this succinctly when he writes:

> in our fascination with Stoker's life and times, there is always the presumption of our own present-day superiority, our ability to know better than our historical precursors. *Dracula*'s continuing circulation in contemporary popular culture depends upon and sustains a powerful representation of the past as a domain of scandal and error, awaiting exposure by a franker, more enlightened gaze.[24]

This does not mean that the psychoanalytical method – for all its contentiousness and the problems it raises – cannot help us in understanding the novel *Dracula* and its adaptations. But it does seem that something more is required, an approach attuned as much to the differences between versions of *Dracula* as to what they all might have in common, an approach more alert both to the mutabilities of history and to the creative work involved in keeping *Dracula* alive from one decade to the next.

THE COMMERCIAL LIFE OF *DRACULA*

'And, too, it made me think of the wonderful power of money! What can it not do when it is properly applied; and what might it do when basely used' (Bram Stoker's *Dracula*).[25] Mina Harker's words highlight a feature of Stoker's novel that is often neglected in psychoanalytical accounts, namely the importance to it of money. To a certain extent, Stoker's 'Crew of Light' defeat Dracula because – as good members of the bourgeoisie and upper class – they are better at spending, or rather investing, money, than the aristocrat vampire who, in one memorable scene, allows his money to spill wastefully from his pocket on to the floor.[26] Stoker himself was very much a man of the commercial theatre and well aware of the financial and exploitative possibilities of *Dracula*. Not long after the novel's publication, he had arranged a public reading of the book on the Lyceum Theatre stage as a way of securing theatrical copyright. The irony of this is that the subsequent history of *Dracula* adaptations can be told largely in terms of disputes over copyright and ownership, with the critical question not so much, 'What is the meaning of *Dracula*?' as it is, 'To whom does *Dracula* belong?' Seeing *Dracula* in this way, as a vulgarly commercial property, is a useful antidote to those more mythic accounts which tend to portray the vampire as emerging from mass culture independent of the will and intention of the film-makers and other cultural agents concerned. It can also give us a sense of the ways in which the *Dracula* narrative has been reworked in order to make it relevant to and valuable for different markets and different contexts.

It has been reported that the first cinematic adaptation of *Dracula* appeared in Hungary in 1920. If such a film did exist – and it is by no means certain that it did – it was not circulated much outside its country of origin. Considering what happened two years later to the producers of *Nosferatu*, an unauthorised German *Dracula* adaptation, this was probably just as well for whatever Hungarian film-makers were involved in the earlier project. The history of the legal hounding of *Nosferatu* by Florence Stoker, Bram's widow, has been recorded by David Skal in his excellent book *Hollywood Gothic*.[27] As Skal notes, the decidedly mercurial production set-up for *Nosferatu*, which included film director Friedrich Wilhelm Murnau, was probably not going far anyway, but Florence Stoker's opposition to this adaptation of her husband's work did not help, and Prana Films, the company in question, was soon consigned to the bankruptcy courts.

Nosferatu turns out to be a very loose adaptation indeed – its story-line, characters and character names differ from those in the novel. In fact, if the original advertising for the film had not mentioned the word 'Dracula', it is possible that no one would ever have noticed that it was an adaptation of a pre-existing source. Perhaps because of F. W. Murnau's subsequent critical reputation, *Nosferatu* has been slightly overvalued over the years. Its most memorable feature – the portrayal of the vampire himself – is also its most problematic. As Graf Orlok (i.e. Count Dracula), the appropriately named Max Schreck (Schreck is the German word for terror) is the most grotesque of all vampires, with his elongated, animal-like fangs, his cadaverous demeanour and his unnervingly erect walk. As Roger Dadoun notes: 'His face is pointed, so are his ears, his shoulders, his knees, his back and of course his nails and fangs ... Nosferatu is an agglomeration of points.'[28] Without doubt, this is a visually impressive undead, but perhaps its grotesqueness is too extreme, too repellent for the drama in which it appears. For instance, one cannot help wondering why it is that Hutter (the film's version of Harker), when confronted with this utter monstrosity, does not im-mediately run screaming from the castle. This Orlok is a world away from Stoker's original Count who could pass, initially at least, as an acceptable host to Jonathan Harker, and it is not a representation of the vampire that has had much influence on subsequent vampire films, other than Werner Herzog's 1979 remake (featuring Klaus Kinski as the vam-pire), the television film *Salem's Lot* (1979), the Francis Coppola-directed *Bram Stoker's Dracula* (1992) and *Shadow of the Vampire* (2000), a fantasy about the making of Murnau's original film that posited that Max Schreck was himself a real vampire.

What was to become the dominant representation of Dracula was being formed elsewhere during the 1920s, first in Britain and then in America. In the early 1920s, Florence Stoker had given permission to Hamilton Deane, a British actor-manager, to write and produce a theat-rical adaptation of her husband's novel. The resulting play performed well in the provinces from 1924 onwards before opening to a successful run in London's West End in February 1927, with the Count played by

2. *Peter Cushing as Van Helsing.*

British actor Raymond Huntley. The play was subsequently revised by London-based American writer John Balderston for an American production that opened in New York in October 1927 with a little-known Hungarian actor by the name of Bela Lugosi in the role of Count Dracula.[29] It was this play, rather than the original Deane version or, for that matter, Stoker's novel, that was adapted for the screen by director Tod Browning at Universal Studios in 1931. The film version of *Dracula*, starring Bela Lugosi, was released in February 1931 and became a huge commercial success that helped to inaugurate the 1930s horror film boom.

The image of Dracula that all this adaptive activity generated was one that very quickly appears to have caught the public's imagination and even today to a certain extent defines what Dracula should look like. It is Dracula as the pale man in the cloak, as the lounge lizard, as the charming but deadly lover with the hypnotic eyes.[30] It has become commonplace for writings on *Dracula* to acknowledge that most people's knowledge of the Count comes not from Stoker's novel but instead from vampire movies. Certainly it might come as a shock to a reader of Stoker's novel who was more accustomed to the cinematic vampire to discover that the novel's Dracula is an old man with 'a long white moustache'[31] who has a 'lofty domed forehead, and hair growing scantily round the temples, but profusely elsewhere',[32] with hair on the palms of his hands as well. This reader might also be surprised by the idea that Dracula becomes more youthful as the story progresses, unless, that is, he or she had seen Jesus Franco's *El Conde Dracula* (1969) or *Bram Stoker's Dracula*. It seems from this that cinema's predominant image of Dracula is as distant from Stoker's original as was Murnau's Graf Orlok.

The other principal legacy of the Deane/Balderston adaptation was its severe truncation of the *Dracula* narrative. For reasons of economy, Deane simply removed the Transylvanian scenes that occur at the beginning and at the end of the novel. The 1931 film restored the opening Transylvanian sequence but did not include the novel's climactic return to Castle Dracula.[33] Deane also initiated something that would later become standard practice for *Dracula* adaptations, namely a reduction in the significance (and sometimes the number of) the four young men who, as 'the Crew of Light', confronted and defeated the Count. Stoker's reliance on what in effect was a collective hero posed problems for stage and film fictions more used to dealing with a single heroic protagonist, problems Deane solved by making one of these young men a female character, while others (including the Hammer film-makers) removed some of these men and marginalised others.

Strictly speaking, the next film adaptation of *Dracula* to appear after the 1931 version was Hammer's 1958 production starring Christopher Lee as the Count.[34] However, Dracula himself as a character would feature sporadically in American films of the 1930s, 1940s and 1950s, although given his status as a major movie monster, it is striking how rarely he or other vampires show up. Mad scientists abound but vampires are surprisingly thin on the ground until Hammer comes along.

The first sequel to *Dracula* was *Dracula's Daughter* which did not appear until 1936. It began where *Dracula* ended, with the staking of the Count by Van Helsing. Thereafter Dracula himself is glimpsed only briefly – in the form of a dummy clearly modelled on Bela Lugosi – before being consigned to the flames by his daughter who then becomes the film's main character. The Count's next, and considerably more substantial, appearance was in *Son of Dracula* (1944) where he was played by Lon Chaney Junior, an actor associated more with the role of the Wolfman.[35] The film, which tells of the Count's arrival in America, is decidedly vague about whether this vampire is actually Dracula's offspring or Dracula himself. (Not for the first time in horror history, a title turns out to be potentially misleading.) In any event, the usual critical response to Chaney's performance has been that it did not work because Chaney was cast against type. One presumes here that the 'type' is the Bela Lugosi type, and certainly Chaney is bulkier and altogether more American than Lugosi could ever have been. Having said this, he is probably no more distant from Stoker's original conception than either Lugosi or Max Schreck, and if he seems 'wrong' in the role, it is because the Deane/Balderston/Lugosi view of Dracula had secured such dominance that it was hard to imagine any other way of showing the vampire.

As if themselves realising how far they had deviated from audience expectations, the Universal film-makers subsequently cast John Carradine as Dracula in *House of Frankenstein* (1944) and *House of Dracula* (1945). Tall, sepulchral and looking good in a cloak, Carradine was much closer to the Lugosi type than was Lon Chaney Junior, although, like Chaney, he did not have what by the mid-1940s had become the irritating distraction of Lugosi's foreign accent. Characteristically for 1940s Universal horror, both *House of Frankenstein* and *House of Dracula* featured several monsters together – with Dracula jostling for screen time with the Wolfman and Frankenstein's monster – and also had deceptive titles; Frankenstein does not appear in *House of Frankenstein*, and while there is a house in *House of Dracula*, it is certainly not Dracula's house nor does the Count have a house in the familial sense of that term.[36] The same can be said for Universal's final *Dracula* film, the horror-comedy *Abbott and Costello Meet Frankenstein* (1948). As with *House of Frankenstein*, Frankenstein himself does not appear, but Dracula is present along with the Wolfman and the Mummy. Significantly, the Count is played here by Bela Lugosi in what would be his second and final cinema appearance in the role. While Lugosi's reappearance as the Count in the last film in the Universal *Dracula* cycle helps to bring that cycle to a neat conclusion, Lugosi himself had previously kept the 'authentic' Dracula image in the public eye by appearing as a Dracula-like vampire in *Mark of the Vampire* (1935) and *The Return of the Vampire* (1943). Neither of these was a Universal production and for copyright reasons Lugosi had been billed as Count Mora in *Mark of the Vampire* and Armand Tesla in *The Return of the Vampire*. However, this had not stopped Universal from attempting unsuccessfully to prevent the release of *Mark of the Vampire*, presumably on the grounds that while he might be called Count Mora, the character played by Lugosi looked, dressed and spoke like the Universal Dracula to the extent that in effect he was the Universal Dracula. (In the sort of self-reflexive twist that we now associate more with modern horror but which is actually quite common throughout the history of horror generally, Count Mora turns out in the film to be an actor pretending to be a vampire rather than the genuine undead article.) Years later, this squabble over the ownership of a particular image of Dracula would take a macabre turn when the wife and son of Lugosi, who famously had gone to the grave dressed in his Dracula cloak, sued Universal unsuccessfully in order to gain control of the proprietary rights to Lugosi's image.[37] If nothing else, the case demonstrated that in the history of *Dracula* adaptation, ownership is everything; and the Hammer film-makers did well to sign a deal with Universal before embarking on their own production of *Dracula*.[38]

In a survey of nineteenth-century vampire stories, Christopher Frayling has observed that: 'The vampire story is gradually "domesticated" throughout the century; as a parallel development, the genre (which became respectable when associated with medieval or classical legends) tends more and more to be set in the "present".'[39] Stoker's novel can clearly be seen as a late-nineteenth-century culmination of this, with its contemporary setting and its overwhelming concern with domestic–familial issues. One might add that the *Dracula* films associated with the Lugosi type take these 'domesticating' and updating tendencies even further in the twentieth century. The Deane/Balderston play was not set in the 1890s but in the 1920s, and its conception of Dracula was, according to David J. Skal, 'a remarkably domesticated one, an image almost perversely sanitized'.[40] Both the 1931 *Dracula* and *Dracula's Daughter* appear to be set in or near the period in which they were made. As if to stress its own modernity and using an idea initially proposed for the 1931 *Dracula*, the vampire in *Dracula's Daughter* escapes to Transylvania by plane, while in the later *Son of Dracula* the Count travels by car and train. The first two multi-monster films, *House of*

Frankenstein and *House of Dracula*, are less obviously 'up-to-date', perhaps because of their European settings, but contain enough references to modern-day dress and modern technology not to be thought of as straightforward period dramas; the Abbott and Costello film, by contrast, is very obviously set in contemporary America. Even the non-Dracula vampire films, *Mark of the Vampire* and *The Return of the Vampire*, are set in or near the present, particularly *The Return of the Vampire* which takes place during the Second World War.

Dracula himself emerges from this as an increasingly anachronistic and out-of-place figure in relation to the characters around him. At the same time he is also someone who seems constantly to be moving closer to the American household as time passes. On one level, this Dracula represents a threat to American domesticity, but on another level, perhaps a more significant one, he becomes a reassuring part of that domesticity, with this most obviously culminating in the popular seasons of horror films that began to be shown on American network television from 1958 onwards. These TV screenings were often introduced by 'horror hosts', macabre figures such as Vampira, Zacherly, Ghoulardi and Tarantula Ghoul, who would make sardonic or sick jokes about the material about to be shown.[41] Framing devices such as these – which in their jokiness reassured viewers that none of this was serious – provided the conduit through which Lugosi's vampire performances, along with many other monster movies and horror movies, made their way into the American home. They were followed in the 1960s by the popular Aurora models of Dracula and other horror monsters that graced the bedrooms of many adolescent boys. It is a reasonable inference that both the familiarity and the pervasiveness of the Lugosi-Dracula in the 1950s and after, and the sense of its having a place within the home, helped to undermine or neutralise any uncanny or disturbing power this representation might once have had.

It is in the nature of genres that they undergo periodic regeneration. Formulas are reworked and stories are retold in attempts to make the genre more attractive to a contemporary audience. To a certain extent, this had been happening in the *Dracula* films from the very beginning: the 1931 film had added material not included in the stage original, subsequent films had offered new Draculas and placed the Count in new locations and alongside other horror monsters. But all these stories had tended not to stray too far from the Lugosi paradigm, even *Son of Dracula* where the physical difference embodied by Lon Chaney Junior had the potential to take the series in another direction. By the late

1950s, this type of film was finding new popularity on television but Universal was no longer making monster movies of this kind and Lugosi himself had died in 1956.

It is within this context that two attempts to update the Dracula format appeared almost simultaneously. One of these was the American-produced *The Return of Dracula* (1958). Made by the same team who had produced *The Vampire* (1957), another vampire story with a contemporary setting, this *Dracula* film was not very successful in its day and is now largely forgotten. It followed the Lugosi tradition in casting a foreigner – Francis Lederer – as the Count who comes to an American town in search of 'new blood'. *The Return of Dracula* owes more than a passing debt to Alfred Hitchcock's thriller *Shadow of a Doubt* (1943) in which a serial killer visits his family in the small town where they live. Some of the vampiric qualities with which Hitchcock invests his killer are in *The Return of Dracula* made literal. Dracula here is not a relative of the family he visits but he is pretending to be a relative, and, as with *Shadow of a Doubt*, it is the children rather than the adults who become suspicious of him. In other ways, *The Return of Dracula* more closely resembles other teen SF/horror films being made at this time, low-budget 'exploitation' projects such as *I was a Teenage Werewolf* (1957), *I was a Teenage Frankenstein* (1957) and *How to Make a Monster* (1958). Such films filled a gap in the market with which the major studios seemed unable or unwilling to engage. *The Return of Dracula* has the same emphasis on the teenage experience as those films as well as the same visual flatness that went with the budgetary restrictions. Seen like this, the film's updating of the vampire turns out to be limited. Certainly the film-makers involved invited the Count into the contemporary American household more emphatically than ever before, but Dracula himself remained firmly in the Lugosi mould and was fairly easily dispatched by the teenagers at the film's conclusion.

The other attempt to update *Dracula* proved considerably more successful. It was, of course, the Hammer *Dracula* of 1958, and it was as distant from *The Return of Dracula* as it possibly could be. Some of these differences have already been noted, but to these can be added now the fact that Hammer's film was the first period *Dracula* since F. W. Murnau's *Nosferatu* in 1922. In less obvious ways, Hammer's film was different from other earlier *Dracula* adaptations – in how it was made, why it was made and, most of all, where it was made. This was the first British *Dracula* since Hamilton Deane's *Dracula* in 1924, and it is worth considering why it was that American cinema, which had maintained such a firm proprietorial grasp on Stoker's creation for three decades, finally in the 1950s passed the property over to a group of unheralded film-makers working at a small studio in Berkshire, England.

THE RISE OF HAMMER

Despite the fact that some key 1930s American horror films were based on British literary sources and used British creative personnel, Britain itself was not a particularly horror-friendly country during the 1930s, at least so far as its film censors were concerned. A new film certificate – 'H' for Horror – had been introduced in the early 1930s as a response to the burgeoning popularity of horror films, but this had not stopped the British Board of Film Classification from heavily cutting some horrors and banning others outright – notably *Freaks* (1932) and *Island of Lost Souls* (1932), the latter a version of H. G. Wells's novel *The Island of Dr Moreau* starring British actor Charles Laughton as the villainous doctor.[42] At a time when screenplays for British films (and sometimes for American films as well) were routinely submitted to the censor prior to the commencement of production, the censor's avowed policy was to discourage horror. As one censor put it in 1935:

> Although a separate category has been established for these films, I am sorry to learn that they are on the increase, as I cannot believe that such films are wholesome, pandering as they do to the love of the morbid and horrible ... Some licensing authorities are already much disturbed about them, and I hope the producers and writers will accept this word of warning, and discourage this type of subject as far as possible.[43]

The outcome of this official disapproval was that during the 1930s very few films were produced in Britain that emulated the American horror formula: probably the only British film of the type still remembered today is *The Ghoul* (1934) which starred British-born Hollywood resident Boris Karloff. In retrospect, one can identify British films from this period that contained Gothic or horror-like elements, notably a series of costume melodramas featuring the hammy performances of Tod Slaughter as well as a number of shocker-thrillers.[44] However, these were not generally perceived as horror at the time (although Graham Greene, not only a novelist but also one of the more perceptive British film critics of the 1930s, claimed that Tod Slaughter's 1939 film *The Face at the Window* 'leaves the American horror films far behind').[45] For British censors, and perhaps for British audiences as well, horror in the

1930s came from abroad, and especially from America. This attitude was maintained during the Second World War to the extent that the import of 'H' films was banned from 1942 to 1945.

All this was to change in the post-war period, with the reasons for this change stemming not just from Britain but also from America. In particular, the break-up of the Hollywood studio system by US anti-trust legislation had implications not just for the American film industry but for parts of the British film industry as well. Up until the late 1940s the major Hollywood studios were vertically integrated, not only producing and distributing their own films but also owning or part-owning the cinemas in which these films were shown. Such a system had clear economic advantages for the studios concerned, but from the perspective of the US government it restricted competition by making it very difficult for independent producers to find outlets for their films. As a result of what came to be known as the Paramount decree of 1948, the major studios were compelled to divest themselves of their cinema chains in order to facilitate the opening up of the industry to competition. This divestment process took place throughout the first half of the 1950s, a period which also saw a significant decline in total audience figures. Coupled with this decline was a shift in the audience demographic, with teenagers becoming an increasingly large sector of the audience.

These changes had several consequences. One was the increased importance in the industry of 'independent' producers (i.e. producers not working for the major studios). Another was the decline of the industry's own censorship practices; as the industry fragmented, the old mechanisms of self-regulation became less effective. As the major studios lost a guaranteed exhibition outlet for their product, they tended to produce fewer films and also concentrated their resources more on expensive and spectacular blockbusters designed to entice people away from their televisions. This in turn led to a shortage of medium- and low-budget product for film exhibitors. As film historian Thomas Doherty has noted, it was at this time, and as a response to the commercial opportunities offered by this situation, that an 'exploitation' cinema began to develop. This consisted of low-budget independent productions often with sensational subjects that 'exploited' relaxed censorship codes and which were directed primarily at teenage audiences.[46]

British cinema in the 1950s never really developed an exploitation sector in the American manner. In part, this was probably because of the relative smallness of the British domestic market, but it also possibly had something to do with the fact that British film exhibition was largely controlled at this time by two companies, Rank and ABC, a situation that sometimes made it difficult for 'independent' producers to prosper. Nevertheless, independent film companies were active in 1950s British cinema, with many of these involved in the production of 60–80-minute films designed to support a main feature. One of the most prolific of these was a small company by the name of Hammer. There had been a Hammer company of sorts briefly in the 1930s – it had produced, among other things, a Bela Lugosi film, *The Mystery of the Marie Celeste* (1935) – but Hammer first appeared as a distinctive entity in the late 1940s as the production arm of a film distributor called Exclusive. For the first few years of its existence, Hammer produced cheap and cheerful support films. Many of these were based on popular BBC radio series, including *Dick Barton – Special Agent* (1947), *Dick Barton at Bay* (1948), *Dick Barton Strikes Back* (1948), *Dr Morelle* (1948), *The Adventures of PC 49* (1949) and *The Man in Black* (1949). Given the ultra-low budgets of these films, and their lack of stars of any magnitude, appealing to an audience's familiarity with pre-existing characters and stories was probably the only reliable marketing device Hammer had.

Nowadays Hammer is usually thought of as a plucky little British company that against all odds managed to achieve unprecedented commercial success, but the change in Hammer's fortunes that occurred in the early 1950s, and which helped set the company on its way to worldwide fame, related more to shifts in the American film industry than it did to anything happening in Britain. In 1951 Hammer negotiated a deal with American independent producer Robert Lippert whereby American stars would appear in Hammer's support features. Mainly these were actors near the end of their careers (for example, George Brent, Paulette Goddard), minor stars such as John Ireland and William Sylvester, or 'stars' that hardly anyone had heard of (Alex Nicol, for instance). Nevertheless, the presence in these films of American accents helped Lippert to market them in the USA at a time when low-budget filler material of this kind was in short supply, and probably also gave the films some additional marquee appeal in the British market. The transatlantic nature of their production context led to the Hammer-Lippert films being considerably less parochial than Hammer's earlier work. Most were thrillers, genre pieces that did not make much of their British settings and which were clearly designed to be comprehensible to both American and British audiences (as opposed to projects like *Dick Barton* or *PC 49* which assumed an already existing familiarity with the British serials from which they were derived).[47]

Throughout the 1950s and 1960s, Hammer proved itself to be a protean and pragmatic company that was perfectly willing to reinvent itself if new market opportunities arose. The Lippert deal would not be the last time in its history that it turned to America for finance, and in the mid-1950s, as the Lippert deal came to an end, it was ready to change direction again. The film that signalled the next step in the company's development turned out to be a science-fiction invasion fantasy, *The Quatermass Experiment* (1955). In certain respects this fitted with Hammer's established way of doing things. It was based on a pre-existing property, Nigel Kneale's ground-breaking BBC TV series, and featured an imported American star in Brian Donlevy. However, in other respects it was quite different. For one thing, it was the first Hammer film to have an X certificate, something that Hammer exploited shamelessly by retitling the film *The Quatermass Xperiment* for its initial release.

The X certificate, which refused admission to anyone under sixteen (raised to eighteen in 1970) had been introduced in the early 1950s. Sometimes seen as a replacement for the H certificate, the X certificate was intended to have a very different function. While 'H' designated something disreputable, 'X' was meant to permit the exhibition of serious 'artistic' films to a discerning adult audience, with the censor particularly interested in the art cinema that was developing across Western Europe in the late 1940s and early 1950s. However, the X certificate quickly became as disreputable as the H certificate had been, and the main cinema circuits, Rank and ABC, generally declined to show such films. In this context, Hammer's producing an X film in 1955 could be seen as both prescient – anticipating as it did the increasing commercial acceptance of the X certificate later on in the 1950s – and more than a little daring. In other ways too, *The Quatermass Experiment* spoke of a certain ambition on the part of Hammer; it had higher production values than previous Hammer films, it made much more of its British settings (including a conclusion in Westminster Abbey), and displayed clear aspirations to be something more than just a support feature.

The commercial success of *The Quatermass Experiment* gave Hammer the opportunity to develop itself further. In part it did this through making films in the same vein as *The Quatermass Experiment*, namely *X – The Unknown* (1956) and *Quatermass II* (1957). However, the more significant change came, as it had done before for Hammer, from America. American producer Milton Subotsky went to Associated Artists

3. *Christopher Lee as Dracula in an awkwardly posed publicity still.*

Pictures in New York with the idea of making a new Frankenstein film. Associated Artists passed the idea over to Hammer, Subotsky left the project (and several years later came to Britain and helped to set up Amicus, a prolific producer of horror films), and, with Associated Artists' financial backing and a distribution deal with Warner Brothers, the Hammer film-makers began work on what would become *The Curse of Frankenstein* (1957), starring Peter Cushing as Frankenstein and featuring Christopher Lee as the Creature.[48] On its release in 1957, *The Curse of*

Frankenstein became a huge commercial success in both Europe and America. According to Thomas Doherty, it 'fathered the most prolific and durable of all '50s exploitation cycles – the horror teenpic', although Doherty also notes that Hammer's production values were considerably higher than those of the American-produced horror teenpics that subsequently flooded the market.[49] He might have added that, unlike most US horror teenpics, Hammer horror from the late 1950s and early 1960s gave no screen space to teenage characters, was set firmly in the past, and contained few American actors. It seems from this that while the development of Hammer throughout the 1950s was intertwined with, and dependent upon, developments within the American film industry, Hammer's horror films were not wholly subsumable, either formally or thematically, within an American exploitation cinema.

In order to grasp what is distinctive about *The Curse of Frankenstein* and later Hammer horrors, it is necessary to have a sense of the Hammer production set-up. Hammer was different from some of the American companies that sprang up in the 1950s to supply the exploitation market; it had been in existence for longer and had developed a continuity in terms of both its personnel and its studio-based resources that was often lacking in those American companies and which facilitated the sort of craftsmanship that Doherty and others have detected in the early Hammer horrors. Hammer had been based at Bray Studio, a small country house converted into a film-making facility, since 1951 and had already produced over fifty films, mainly at Bray but occasionally elsewhere, before it turned to horror. In that time it had also built up an experienced team of technicians and creative personnel who would be important to the later horrors – including director Terence Fisher, screenwriter Jimmy Sangster, producers Michael Carreras (the grandson of one of Hammer's founders, Enrique Carreras) and Anthony Hinds (the son of Hammer's other founder, William Hinds; Anthony Hinds would also write screenplays for the company under the name 'John Elder'), editor James Needs and production designer Bernard Robinson. What this meant was that the team that produced *The Curse of Franken-stein* were film-makers of 'the old school', with many years of experience working together within the industry behind them, and firmly committed to industrial standards of professionalism and quality.

The Curse of Frankenstein reflects this experience. It is a solidly 'well-made' film, a work characterised by measured camerawork, a strongly linear narrative, and surprisingly high production values for its low budget. Its moments of violence and gore – which shocked some British critics so much on the film's initial release – are all the more striking for the way in which they stand out from the decidedly sober background provided by director Terence Fisher and his collaborators.

A number of critics have since seen *The Curse of Frankenstein* as beginning to articulate a new viewpoint for British cinema. After what is often perceived as the predominant social conformism of British film entertainment in the first part of the 1950s, Hammer horror's privileging of the individual, and an accompanying emphasis on sexuality, points to another way of thinking about the relation between the individual and the community/nation. Baron Frankenstein might be a monster in *The Curse of Frankenstein*, but he is a supremely attractive and dynamic monster, particularly when opposed to the boring moralistic strictures offered by the forces of normality in the film. In this he might be seen as an aristocratic precursor of the aggressively individualistic working-class heroes who would populate the British New Wave films from the late 1950s onwards and the James Bond films of the early 1960s. Ultimately, however, *The Curse of Frankenstein* retreats from a comprehensively amoral approval of its 'hero'; at the end of the film, Frankenstein, now reduced to a state of quivering fear, awaits execution for his crimes. In the final triumph of morality, *The Curse of Frankenstein* harks back to earlier Universal horrors, although there the deviance of the 'mad scientist' was accentuated much more than in Hammer's first Frankenstein film where the Baron himself is anything but mad.

By the time it turned to horror production, Hammer was already accustomed to producing sequels – from the *Dick Barton* series in the late 1940s to *Quatermass II* in 1957 – and given the success of *The Curse of Frankenstein*, it was inevitable that more horrors were to follow. One of these, a sequel to *The Curse of Frankenstein* to be called *The Revenge of Frankenstein*, went into production in January 1958. But Hammer's next Gothic was not to be a Frankenstein film at all. Instead, in a move reminiscent of the beginnings of Universal horror in the early 1930s when film versions of *Dracula* and *Frankenstein* appeared within a few months of each other, the Hammer film-makers turned their attention to the story of the vampire.

During the production of *The Curse of Frankenstein*, Hammer had been keenly aware of the need to distinguish its version of Frankenstein from the famous Universal–Karloff version. This was not simply in the interests of product differentiation but also to protect themselves from Universal's lawyers, for while Mary Shelley's original Gothic novel was in the public domain, Universal's film was not, and if Hammer had used any story or character elements that were in the Universal version but not in the Shelley novel, it would have been liable to prosecution. Hence in particular Hammer's visualisation of the creature as something quite distinct from the square-headed, neck-bolted Karloff monster.[50]

This threat had been removed by the time of *Dracula*'s production by the simple fact of Universal giving Hammer permission to remake its backlist of horror films. This act, which was not accorded much significance at the time, represented in fact a remarkable acknowledgement by a major American studio that this small British company had a kind of ownership of period horror. Such an acknowledgement was probably possible only because of the fragmentation of the American film industry and that industry's ongoing uncertainty about what its audiences actually wanted. It follows that if this was a case of Gothic horror finally coming home to Britain, it was coming because of economic and industrial reasons rather than simply being an expression of some inner British propensity for the Gothic.

So far as Hammer was concerned, it was business as usual when its team of film-makers assembled on 11 November 1957 to commence production on *Dracula*. Director Terence Fisher, cinematographer Jack Asher, and actors Peter Cushing and Christopher Lee had all worked on *The Curse of Frankenstein*, as had production designer Bernard Robinson, screenwriter Jimmy Sangster, editor James Needs, and composer James Bernard, and *Dracula* was an obvious attempt to exploit the success of that film. The budget had increased, from *The Curse of Frankenstein*'s £64,000 to £81,000, the shooting schedule was slightly longer, and, given *Curse*'s phenomenal commercial success, expectations were probably higher too. That the film which emerged from this situation turned out to be one of the more remarkable British films of the post-war period is a testament to the considerable skills and abilities of the film-makers concerned. Certainly it does seem to have been one of those felicitous productions where all the different elements of the film-making process came together perfectly. How precisely they came together, and to what effect, are questions that now need to be considered. It's time to visit Castle Dracula.

TWO
'I'm Dracula'

Principal photography on Hammer's *Dracula* commenced on 11 November 1957 and concluded on 3 January 1958, and the completed film was premièred in both Britain and America in May 1958. For Hammer in the late 1950s, this was one of its longer schedules, but by any other standards it was a short production period preceded by a short pre-production and followed by a short post-production. The completed film bore all the hallmarks of a low-budget project: a small cast, a small number of locations, no crowd scenes or scenes of elaborate spectacle, some illogicalities in the screenplay, and, along with other films emerging from the low-budget sector of the British film industry at this time, a lack of prestige. As if to confirm its lowly status, Hammer assiduously promoted itself throughout the late 1950s and 1960s as a commercially-minded, market-led company. 'I'm prepared to make Strauss waltzes tomorrow if they'll make money,' the eminently quotable Hammer chief James Carreras once stated.[1] Such an attitude has sometimes been seen as betraying a philistine crassness on the part of the Hammer film-makers, with this then used to damn Hammer's films. A more balanced account might identify this promotion of Hammer's image as simply that, the promotion of an image undertaken to raise the market's awareness of this small, hitherto relatively unknown company. As James Carreras himself put it: 'When I see producers who are reluctant to bang the big drum about their product, it makes me wonder why they bother to make films at all.'[2]

One of the ways in which Hammer sought to create a place for itself in the market in the late 1950s was through investing its product with particular notions of quality. In recent years the term 'quality' has become associated with a type of costume drama usually seen as anti-thetical to Hammer horror: films such as *A Passage to India* (1984), *Room with a View* (1986) and *Howards End* (1991) offer high production values, stylistic restraint, historically accurate detail, and, as adaptations of canonical literary texts, cultural prestige as well. Even to mention such films in the same breath as Hammer horror, in the eyes of some at least, risks besmirching the integrity and value of the 'quality' costume drama/literary adaptation. Nevertheless, Hammer horror films have been perceived as 'quality', both retrospectively – by Thomas Doherty in his book *Teenagers and Teenpics* – and at the time of their initial release.[3] As one critic rather grudgingly noted a few months after the release of the Hammer *Dracula*: 'Hammer has a programme of horrors and thrillers which take it into 1960. Though the company has offended those who take their pictuegoing seriously, there is no doubt it has brought a certain standard of quality to the gimmick subject.'[4] Quality here does not refer to any cultural status but rather to a certain care taken with the production that separated the Hammer films from their generic competitors. As a reader's letter to *Films and Filming* puts it in regard of Hammer's *Dracula*: 'This film is in the Oscar class compared with some of the awful cheap quickie supporting films which have been churned out recently bearing an "X" certificate.'[5]

It seems clear that the Hammer film-makers were in the business of producing not just marketable films but also 'good' films, with this 'goodness' or quality ultimately forming part of the films' distinctiveness in the market. The Hammer approach promoted an attention to detail in production and costume design, camerawork and lighting, performance, editing and music, among other things, and an accompanying concern to push a low budget to its limits, to make a film appear more expensive than it actually was. This in turn invested the films themselves with a degree of energy and ambition, not necessarily an artistic or cultural ambition but instead an ambition to do absolutely the best one could with the material available, for reasons of professional pride if nothing else. In effect, this entailed a commitment to the process of storytelling and the creative transformation of generic formulae and conventions in order to produce new stories and new experiences for audiences. As one might expect, this process was at its most dynamic in the early days of Hammer horror; later, as Hammer maintained a breakneck rate of production, the creativity inevitably faltered, and the films themselves began to fall back on established formulae.

Hammer's *Dracula* represents both the boldest and the most balanced product of the 'classic' period of Hammer horror, 1957–64. It has the production values and many of the virtues of the 'well-made film', it has the invention and the innovation, and, most of all, it has the energy. In fact, energy is the key to understanding how this *Dracula* is different from previous *Dracula* films. As opposed to the rather somnolent pacing of the 1931 *Dracula*, Hammer's film progresses at speed, with this manifesting itself in a rapid narrative development, in restless camerawork, and in the physical actions of the characters as they move, masterfully or fearfully but always dynamically, through the world conjured up by the film-makers. Notions of transformation are also important in identifying what it is that makes the Hammer *Dracula* special. The transformation from one state to another is viewed here as a dynamic process involving the expenditure of energy, whether this be the change from day to night (or night to day), from human to vampire, or, finally, from vampire to pile of dust.

What follows is an account of the energy and power of the Hammer *Dracula*. It is tempting to make claims for the film's 'artistic' status (perhaps by putting a case for director Terence Fisher as auteur, or connecting the film to a venerable Gothic tradition) or to view it as symptomatic of broader cultural and institutional factors. While both of these approaches will undoubtedly creep into my account at certain points, I prefer in the main to see *Dracula* in its own terms, as a repository of the film-makers' skills, experiences and ambitions and as a vital expression of their creative drive and energy. For those more accustomed to viewing Hammer's films through the company's public image, this might seem an odd way of proceeding. For me, it is the best way of grasping what is valuable about this particular adaptation of *Dracula*.

OVERTURE

In retrospect, there is something tentative about the opening of Hammer's first Gothic horror film, *The Curse of Frankenstein* (1957). A pre-credit caption informs us that 'More than a hundred years ago, in a mountain village in Switzerland, lived a man whose strange experiments with the dead have since become legend.' This is followed by credits in Gothic type against a blood-red background. The opening sequence then shows a priest arriving at a prison where he meets Baron Frankenstein, a prisoner awaiting execution. The Baron proceeds to tell him the story of his creation of life, and the narrative finally commences. It is as if the film-makers themselves are uncertain what tone to adopt in a film that was unlike anything Hammer had ever produced before, hence the captions and some other unwieldy exposition.

The opening sequence of *Dracula*, Hammer's second Gothic horror and made in the wake of the extraordinary success of *The Curse of*

Frankenstein, is strikingly different. It is brasher, louder, bolder, innovative, more confident, more cinematic. It has no equivalent in either Stoker's *Dracula* or in any subsequent *Dracula* adaptation and, as we will see, it is also unusual so far as the horror genre in general is concerned.

We begin with a low angle shot of a statue of a bird perched on a pedestal, with a high wall in the background. It is a bird of prey, perhaps a hawk; and the camera views it from one side, at an angle of approximately 45 degrees. The film's credits appear, in red Gothic type, over this statue. As the screenplay credit – 'by Jimmy Sangster' – comes up, the camera starts to move, tracking slowly from left to right and panning slightly from right to left to keep the stone bird in frame.[6] As the credits conclude with Terence Fisher's directorial credit, the right-to-left pan continues until the statue disappears from view (although we can see an identical statue up ahead on the right). The camera is now pointing back in the direction from which it came, and for the first time we can see what appears to be the entrance to a building. The camera then tracks back the way it has come while the leftwards pan continues until we can no longer see the entrance. Another door, smaller this time, comes into view at the bottom of a short flight of stairs.

Fade.

We are inside a cellar-like room, presumably that which lies beyond the door seen at the end of the previous shot. The camera tracks through the room towards a tomb which bears the name-plate DRACULA. As the name-plate fills the screen, blood spatters on to it from an unseen source.

Fade to black.

This short sequence runs less than two minutes but its apparent simplicity should not obscure the various ways in which the camerawork conveys to us not just an environment – the exterior of Castle Dracula – but also an attitude to that environment and to the drama that is about to begin.

On the most basic level, the audience is being manipulated here into believing that the set is much bigger than it actually is. Later in the film, when the set is shown again, this time in long-shot, we can see that the statue and the cellar door are in fact only a few feet apart, and to move from one to the other should only take a few seconds. The camera takes so long to make the journey because it is moving both slowly and via an indirect route. The combination of a left-to-right/right-to-left track and an approximate 225-degree pan has the effect of expanding space to the extent that we seem to be travelling for ever before we reach our destination while in actuality the camera moves hardly any distance at all. Most of the Hammer film-makers had spent their careers working in small, cramped studios and had grown accustomed to making the most of minimal resources; the abilities and skills involved in this are key to Hammer's status in the market as 'quality' horror. In the case of Hammer horror in particular, Bernard Robinson's set designs often managed to convey a sense of the spacious on a tiny budget while director Terence Fisher – who directed most of the classic Hammer horrors, including *The Curse of Frankenstein* and *Dracula* – knew exactly how to make these sets appear even larger. The technique he uses for the opening of *Dracula* – combining a track with a pan in the opposite direction, and sending the camera on an indirect route that doubles back on itself – is one he deploys elsewhere both in *Dracula* and later Hammer horrors.[7] This opening camera movement also helps to distract the audience both from the modest proportions of the building being filmed and the oddness of some of its features. The entrance to the castle is hardly a grand entrance – especially when compared with the much more spectacular presentation of Castle Dracula in Universal's 1931 version of the story – and, for some unexplained reason, the entrance to the cellar, presumably the place where the Count is at his most vulnerable as he sleeps in his tomb, is located outside the castle's protective walls. However, the opening sequence discourages us from thinking about this and other prosaic matters simply by directing us through the space in a very authoritative manner and not inviting us to linger over any details it does not want us to linger over.

There is more to this opening than an expansion of space, however, for the sequence also seeks to convey the presence of Count Dracula without actually showing us the vampire in person. The first shot begins with an image of a stone hawk over which the title Dracula is imposed. As a haughty and noble predator, the hawk can reasonably be seen as a stand-in for Dracula himself. The camera then moves inexorably, if indirectly, towards the door beyond which we discover Dracula's tomb. Again Dracula himself is absent, with only a name-plate to indicate that this is where the vampire once was. Finally, as the camera moves close to the tomb's name-plate, blood falls upon it from above. We do not see the source of this blood, and given that only a few seconds before the cellar was apparently empty, we do not know for certain what this source is. Nevertheless, we suspect it is Dracula, a shadowy presence lurking ominously offscreen.

Film historian Gregory Waller makes two interesting points about this sequence. The first is that the contrast between the grey hues of the cellar and the bright redness of the blood is Hammer's way of under-lining the fact that the most distinctive feature of its horror, in the late 1950s at least, is its colour.[8] Throughout *Dracula*, cinematographer Jack Asher makes skilful use of Eastman Color, which in the late 1950s was a relatively cheap and rather crude photographic process, to produce a vivid palette of deep reds and blues, colours which lend themselves in the tomb sequence to what is essentially a shock effect and which else-where contribute enormously to the film's mood. Critic Nina Auerbach has gone so far as to compare the pattern made by the blood on the tomb with a Jackson Pollock painting.[9] While this reading might initially seem rather fanciful, seeing the sequence as a piece of abstract expres-sionism does make some sense so far as its function in the film is concerned, and it also leads us neatly to Waller's second point which is that the sequence as a whole is all the more disturbing for having no apparent connection with the narrative that follows.[10]

The fact that the sequence is not exposition in the conventional sense of that term does not mean that it is not motivated in other ways, especially where the film's generic identity is concerned. American horror in the 1930s and 1940s had developed a propensity for expressive and sometimes extravagant camerawork that often went beyond the immedi-ate needs of the narrative to evoke mood and atmosphere. One thinks here, to give just two examples, of the 'creation' scene in *The Bride of Frankenstein* (1935) and the heroine's night-time journey to the voodoo ceremony in *I Walked with a Zombie* (1943). To a certain extent, the opening sequence of *Dracula* does precisely what these other sequences do; it evokes a particular mood, a mood of ominous foreboding. Some-thing evil and powerful is lurking here, the sequence is telling us, something that will eventually appear to threaten us. But even by the standards of the horror genre, and especially film horror in the 1950s, the *Dracula* sequence is excessive. The opening sequences of *The Curse of Frankenstein* and other horror films of the late 1950s, such as *I was a Teenage Werewolf* (1957) and *I was a Teenage Frankenstein* (1957), are more prosaic and functional, to the extent that they might be deemed to be in some sense realistic. If one goes back as far as the 1931 *Dracula*, there is a sequence near the beginning of the film in which the camera moves slowly through what appears to be a dungeon towards Dracula's coffin. In contrast, the opening of Hammer's *Dracula* is lengthier, offers a more dramatic track/pan combination and is more emphatically sealed off from the rest of the film.[11] A better comparison might be with the openings of Alfred Hitchcock's *Rebecca* (1940) and Orson Welles's *Citizen Kane* (1941). In each of these, a camera moves 'magically' through boundaries (as in *Dracula* we seem to pass magically through the cellar door) in order to explore an unknown, mysterious space, in the case of *Rebecca* the ruined, overgrown estate of Manderley and in *Citizen Kane* the palatial home of the enigmatic Charles Foster Kane. One might balk at comparing these films, both the work of illustrious and critically revered directors, with a low-budget horror film, even a well-made one. Putting aside (for the moment at least) the comparative artistic merits of these three films, it should at least be acknowledged that their openings all rely on the ability of the camera to move us forwards into a space in a manner that gives a sense of great power. This power is not our power, however, but rather the power of the film-makers over us, their ability to take an audience anywhere they want it to go. So, ultimately, what the opening sequence of *Dracula* does with its long, purposeful camera movements is dramatise the film-makers' authority and our subjection to that authority. As will become apparent later in this chapter, this conjunction of authority and subjection is one that organises the interaction of characters within the film. In this respect, *Dracula*'s beginning can be seen not just as an atmospheric overture but as a thematic one as well.

The other significant element introduced in this opening sequence is composer James Bernard's musical score. As is well-known by now, to Hammer aficionados at least, the three-note Dracula theme that plays over the credits – with one sustained note followed by two repeated lower notes – is designed in its intonation to mimic the word 'Dra-cu-la'. While one would not necessarily expect an audience to notice this, it could be argued that the theme does function here as a subliminal reminder of Dracula himself, and in this it can be aligned with the stone hawk and the empty tomb as another stand-in for his presence.[12]

Bernard had already written scores for *The Quatermass Experiment* (1955: his first film score after composing mainly for television), *X – The Unknown* (1956), *The Curse of Frankenstein* and *Quatermass II* (1957), and he would go on to write the music for many other Hammer horrors. His compositional style, which involved an extensive use of brass and percussion, would prove important in helping to form Hammer horror's distinctiveness, and it was also of some significance in the history of horror film music in general. Despite its antecedents in 1920s American and European cinema, the horror film genre has often been seen by historians as beginning in an organised way in the early 1930s. Like other popular genres from that period, such as the musical and the gangster film, horror sought to explore and exploit the possibilities of new sound-on-film technology, which for horror meant not just the sound of screams, of wolves howling and doors creaking, but also music. However, early horrors had generally used music in an unadventurous manner – the 1931 *Dracula* had featured largely pre-existing classical music, for example – and the horror genre had to wait until 1935 for its first memorable score, Franz Waxman's music for *The Bride of Frankenstein*.[13] Thereafter music had an important part to play in 1930s and 1940s horror so far as the evocation of mood and suspense was concerned, although this music tended not to be particularly distinctive in its own right. It is not unreasonable in this respect to see Bernard's music for *Dracula* as horror's second truly memorable signature score after *The Bride of Frankenstein* (with due commendation for the less impressive but still effective score for *The Curse of Frankenstein*). From the late 1950s onwards, the idea that a horror film should have its own distinctive musical signature became more important in the genre, and scores appeared that were more ambitious, that drew attention to themselves as elements in particular films, and that sometimes had a life beyond the films in which they initially appeared. One thinks here, to give just a few examples, of Bernard Herrmann's score for Hitchcock's *Psycho* (1960), Krzysztof Komeda's lullaby theme for Roman Polanski's *Rosemary's Baby* (1968), Ennio Morricone's and rock group Goblin's scores for the Italian horror films of Dario Argento, Jerry Goldsmith's choral work for *The Omen* trilogy, and director John Carpenter's theme for his own *Halloween* (1978).

For such a small and commercially-minded company, Hammer had a surprisingly sophisticated music policy in the late 1950s and early 1960s, frequently giving opportunities to classically-trained composers with little or no experience of writing film music – composers such as Franz Reizenstein (*The Mummy*), Richard Rodney Bennett (*The Man Who Could Cheat Death*, *The Witches*), Benjamin Frankel (*The Curse of the Werewolf*) and Malcolm Williamson (*The Brides of Dracula*) as well as, of course, James Bernard, and the scores themselves showed a level of ambition and sophistication not much seen in the horror genre up until this point. Hammer's contribution to the development of horror film music has rarely been recognised, but even by the company's high standards, Bernard's *Dracula* score stands out, both for its inventive use in the film and for its inherent musical quality.[14] What his strident music does for the film's opening sequence, aside from suggesting the offscreen presence of Dracula, is underline its authoritative nature and impart an urgency to the forward movement of the camera. Equally significant, however, is the music's abrupt cessation just before the sequence's most 'dramatic' moment, the splashing of blood on to the tomb. This sudden and unsettling transition from stridency to silence can be seen as marking the end of authority and the beginnings of doubt and uncertainty, and in this it sets the tone for the next few scenes in the film.

THE WEAKNESS OF JONATHAN HARKER

The next section of the film introduces us to Dracula via Jonathan Harker's encounter with him. There are three stages to this: Harker's arrival at Castle Dracula and his first meeting with the Count; Harker's being attacked by a female vampire; and Harker's attempt to destroy Dracula. Here, the Hammer film-makers engage for the first time with a perennial issue in vampire fiction, namely that the idea of a creature returning from the dead in order to suck the blood of the living is not one that attracts much belief in our modern world. The appeal of the vampire, then, is based firmly in fantasy. Yet vampire fictions have often played with the vampire's implausibility, making it part of the drama by presenting us with rational 'non-believers' who in the course of a narrative are compelled to accept the existence of vampires. In Stoker's *Dracula*, the initial rational perspective is provided by Jonathan Harker, an English solicitor who travels to Transylvania in order to close a property deal with Count Dracula. Sinister events in Dracula's castle turn Harker into a believer in the Count's monstrosity, and, on his eventual return to England, he willingly joins the fight against the vampire. This transition from disbelief to belief is subsequently repeated elsewhere in the novel for several characters, with much of this orchestrated by charismatic arch-believer Abraham Van Helsing.

By the time we get to the 1931 Universal film of *Dracula*, the emphasis has changed. There is still a disbeliever visiting the castle, although this time it is Renfield, who was an asylum inmate in Stoker's novel, rather than Harker. In contrast to Stoker's novel where Harker is a sensible individual with whom we are meant to identify, the 1931 Renfield is presented as gullible to the point of idiocy as he blithely ignores the warnings issued by local peasants and blunders cheerfully into the ultra-sinister castle. (In this respect, he is not unlike the oafish Hutter/Harker in Murnau's 1922 film *Nosferatu*.) The diminution in stature of the first visitor to Castle Dracula traced in the movement from Stoker's novel to the 1931 film arguably reflects the growing popularity of *Dracula* in the

1920s. It is worth remembering that the film was based on a successful stage play, and the film-makers, unlike Stoker, could assume that their audience would be familiar with the idea of Dracula the vampire. It follows that a character in the 1930s who professed to know nothing about vampires (we are not talking about belief in vampires here, just knowledge of them) would be less of an identification figure than he would be in an 1897 novel. Bearing this in mind, it is perhaps appropriate that the Universal film-makers cast Renfield, Stoker's lunatic, in this role and later in the film have him collapse into insanity.

By the time the Hammer film-makers turned to the story of the vampire in the late 1950s, Dracula was yet more familiar to audiences, and the disparity between the audience's knowledge of vampires and the fictional characters' knowledge was even more marked than it had been for the Universal *Dracula* in 1931. Hammer's response was, ostensibly at least, a fairly conventional one, returning to the novel for its opening scenes and, for the first time in cinema since Murnau's *Nosferatu* in 1922, showing Jonathan Harker's encounter with Dracula (although Hammer's Harker is not a solicitor but instead a librarian come to catalogue the Count's books). On another level, however, Hammer was playing with its audience's expectations and doing so in a manner that is still effective today.

'The diary of Jonathan Harker. 3 May 1885.' As we hear Harker's voiceover, we are given a close-up of the diary itself. On one level, this rather old-fashioned expository device refers back to the novel which also begins with entries in Harker's diary; but on another level, the distinctiveness of this version of *Dracula* is subtly being signalled here. For one thing, this is a *Dracula* set firmly in the past, set in fact twelve years before the publication of Stoker's novel. Gone are all the dramatic possibilities involved in a representative of the new world meeting someone who belongs to the old world, possibilities explored in earlier *Dracula* films and plays. In addition, Harker's first diary entry, presumably written on the journey to Castle Dracula, turns out to be not as 'innocent' as it might initially seem, and Harker himself far more prepared for Dracula than any of his literary or cinematic predecessors.

At first glance, Harker as revealed by his first diary entry does appear to be the stereotypically unsuspecting victim. His voiceover notes that the coachman would not take him close to the castle, that no birds sing in the area, and that the temperature drops as he enters the castle grounds, but despite these sinister portents, he approaches the castle with no apparent anxiety. However, some of his early comments are decidedly

4. *Dracula (Christopher Lee) visits the Holmwood house.*

ambiguous. 'At last my long journey is drawing to its close. What the eventual end will be I cannot foresee, but whatever may happen, I can rest secure that I will have done all in my power to achieve success,' he states solemnly and concludes his first diary entry by announcing that he 'did not intend to falter in my purpose'. These are unduly dramatic words from a librarian about to catalogue some books, but the quietness of the voiceover, and the fact that it is presented in the form of a private diary entry rather than as a public statement, encourages us to take it at face value rather than as a piece of dissimulation. Accordingly, an unsuspecting audience is made to feel superior to Harker; we feel that that we know more than Harker about what awaits him in the castle.

In effect, what this part of the sequence does is set up the audience, luring it into a false sense of its own superiority only in order to overthrow it later on. This is perhaps why a scene showing the last part of Harker's coach trip to the castle was not included in the finished film. (There is some doubt whether the scene was actually filmed, although the fact that actors had been signed up for it suggests that it was.) In the scene, various superstitious locals warn Harker about impending danger, in much the same way as Hutter and Renfield are warned about vampires in *Nosferatu* (1922) and *Dracula* (1931). In these earlier films, Hutter/ Renfield's disregarding of these warnings had emphasised his own foolishness. By contrast, the Hammer film-makers were obviously keen to avoid showing Harker as foolish or ignorant for reasons that would become apparent later in the film, and by removing this scene they maintained him as an apparently innocent but in reality rather ambiguous figure.

The visuals that accompany Harker's voiceover are as low-key as the diary entry itself. There is a long-shot of a carriage driving down a country road (presumably a remnant of the deleted scene) then a cut to Harker as he approaches the castle on foot. He passes through the same entranceway that only a few minutes before, in the film's credit sequence, had seemed both so grand and so menacing but which now – filmed in static long- and medium-shots – seems considerably less imposing. He does not even look at the statuary birds and only glances at the cellar door before moving on (although, like so much else in this part of the film, that glance becomes more significant in retrospect). Then he enters the castle itself.

Anyone familiar with the castle in the 1931 *Dracula* is likely to be surprised by the relatively modest dimensions of the Hammer castle. As opposed to the cavernous ruins of Lugosi's abode, which is full of spiders' webs and has armadillos roaming inside and wolves howling outside, this castle is clean, tidy and comfortable, more like a country house than a Gothic dwelling. In fact, Dracula himself never refers to it as a castle but instead describes it as a house and his home. The only outré details are the cannon briefly glimpsed outside the castle's entrance and the ornate arches through which Harker passes in the castle's entrance hall. Of course, the lack of spectacle in the film's production design can be attributed to Hammer's limited budget, but, as they do elsewhere in the film, the Hammer film-makers make a positive use of these limitations. By cutting the castle down to size, and later in the film compressing the geographical scope of Stoker's novel, they perpetuate the domestication of Dracula going on elsewhere in popular culture in the 1950s.[15] At the same time, however, they manage to reconfigure this in such a way that Dracula himself becomes a more disturbing figure, disturbing not despite his being closer to home but rather because of it.

In comparison with the dramatic tension and bloodshed of the film's credits sequence, the scene where Harker waits for Dracula to arrive seems mundane in the extreme. Harker walks into the dining hall and finds a note from the Count inviting him to 'Eat well, make yourself comfortable' and a meal already laid out. Harker proceeds to make himself comfortable – not something that would have been possible in Lugosi's unwelcoming castle – and, after a fade signifying that time has passed he is shown to be still obediently seated there. Even here, however, amidst this scene of apparent domestic contentment, there are subtle indications of something amiss. In particular, the shot where Harker enters the hall turns out to be a variation of the one that opened the film – in this instance, a right-to-left track combined with a pan in the opposite direction. There is something quietly unnerving about this shot, not only in that it refers back to that earlier more sinister shot but also because its elaborate nature seems excessive in relation to what is actually being filmed, i.e. Harker walking across a room. In addition to this, Harker's 'passivity' is becoming both more obvious and more distracting. Already he has ignored all the signs that this is not a normal building, and now he sits patiently inside the castle, showing no interest at all in his surroundings.

Then, finally, something happens. Harker accidentally knocks a metal plate off the table and bends down to pick it up. As he does so, a woman dressed in what passes in the late 1950s for a flimsy negligée appears behind him. Harker turns, sees her, smiles and speaks the first lines of dialogue in the film: 'I'm sorry. I didn't hear you come in. My name's Jonathan Harker. I'm the new librarian.' These undramatic words are at one with the deliberately slow-paced and low-key quality of Harker's entrance into the castle. But the woman's appearance – in particular the sexualised nature of her costume – and her response to Harker's words change the tone and introduce new complications. 'You will help me, won't you?' she asks Harker as she moves closer and then goes on to accuse Dracula of imprisoning her in the castle.

From our present-day perspective, this character's seductive manner clearly marks her as a potential vampire, someone of whom one should be wary. In this respect, Harker's not being suspicious of her is merely another indicator of his inadequacy. However, for an audience in the late 1950s, the situation was not as transparent, for this woman does not really resemble any of the images of female vampirism available to that audience. Earlier female vampires – and there are not many in 1930s and 1940s horror cinema – tended to be ethereal, ghost-like creatures such as Dracula's three brides in *Dracula* (1931), Carol Borland's Luna in *Mark of the Vampire* (1935), or Countess Zaleska in *Dracula's Daughter* (1936). The woman encountered by Harker in Hammer's *Dracula* is not at all like this. She is a much more solidly physical figure and in addition speaks with an impeccable English accent. The more observant members of the 1950s audience might even have recognised Valerie Gaunt, the actress in the part, from her performance as Justine, a sexy French-accented servant, in *The Curse of Frankenstein*, and simply assumed that she was playing a similar sexy role here. Even Stoker's novel is not much help in identifying this character as a vampire, for Stoker's 'brides' do not show up until after Dracula himself has made his appearance and in any event there are three of them rather than, as here, just one. So, in the context of its time, there is little about this character that explicitly signifies vampirism, and the story she tells Harker is, within the terms of the film, not incredible. The audience might have its suspicions – this is Dracula's castle, after all – but there is not enough information available for that audience to be in a superior position of knowledge to Harker so far as this woman is concerned.

Suddenly the woman walks away. Harker looks up and for the first time in the film his face registers surprise. There is a cut to a figure standing in silhouette at the top of the staircase. James Bernard's three-note Dracula theme roars on the soundtrack, and the Count himself moves quickly down the stairs towards Harker. This movement is done in one shot, beginning with Dracula in long-shot and concluding with him in close-up as he speaks to Harker for the first time.

The introduction of Dracula is a crucial moment for any *Dracula* adaptation. It is the moment where a sense of an adaptation's specificity, its relationship with and its difference from prior versions of the tale, can be signalled most clearly. While Hammer's treatment of this moment is clearly modelled on Lugosi's appearance at the head of a grand flight of stairs in the 1931 *Dracula*, the invoking of that earlier film works to distance the Hammer version from it. Terence Fisher, the director of the Hammer *Dracula*, recalls the scene thus:

> In my film, when Dracula made his first appearance, he took a long time to come down the stairs but it seems a short time because you're waiting to see what he's going to look like. Because, the first time, everybody was ready to laugh their bloody heads off – I've seen it in cinemas again and again – they thought they were going to see fangs and everything. They didn't, of course. Instead they saw a charming and extremely good looking man with a touch, an undercurrent of evil or menace.[16]

The raising of expectations only to confound them is one of the main ways in which genres renew themselves. In the case of the Hammer

Dracula, the portrayal of the vampire that would have provoked laughter would have been the one associated with Bela Lugosi, a portrayal that might have been disturbing back in the early 1930s but which by the late 1950s had become familiar to the point of risibility. In visual terms, Christopher Lee as Dracula is very different: taller and more conventionally handsome than Lugosi (or 'tall, dark and gruesome' as Lee's autobiography puts it), and, as quickly becomes apparent, with an English accent as opposed to Lugosi's thick Hungarian tones.[17] However, it is not only the physical differences between Lugosi's and Lee's portrayal of Dracula that separate Hammer's film from its Universal predecessor. Lugosi's famous appearance on the grand staircase, where he announces portentously to Renfield 'I am Dracula', is in fact his third appearance in the film. The first time we see him he has just emerged from his coffin and is staring mesmerically at the camera; the second time he is disguised (although still recognisable) as the coachman who brings Renfield to the castle. It is as if the Universal film-makers felt the need to unveil their Dracula gradually, underscoring his menace prior to Renfield's encounter with him and thereby distancing the audience from Renfield as a potential identificatory figure. In contrast, while the Hammer version offers us some early 'stand-ins' for the Count, Dracula himself remains absent until his decisive appearance on the stairs, with this absence rendering the appearance all the more dramatic and show-stopping. In doing this, Hammer also sets a pattern for the rest of the film whereby Dracula's entrances are usually presented as sudden and often violent intrusions into a range of domestic settings.

Having said this, Dracula's words to Harker immediately restore some decorum: 'Mr Harker, I'm glad that you have arrived safely.' 'Count Dracula?' asks Harker. 'I'm Dracula and I welcome you to my house,' the Count replies, a charming host who carries Harker's bag as he leads his guest upstairs. An audience of the 1950s would have been unaccustomed to such elaborate politeness from its screen vampires: this Dracula can even make small talk, it seems. It is just another aspect of Hammer's systematic suppression of those grotesque elements that had helped to define earlier vampire films but which are here replaced by a smaller-scale and to a certain extent more urbane treatment of the vampire. (Lee's 'I'm Dracula' is considerably more conversational than Lugosi's declamatory 'I am Dracula.')

Deposited in his room and warned by Dracula that he will be away until tomorrow evening, Harker is left to his own devices. Hearing a click from the door, he realises that he has been locked in. He then sits down to write his second diary entry, which turns out to be very different from the first: 'At last I have met Count Dracula. He accepts me as a man who has agreed to work among his books, as I intended. It only remains for me now to await the daylight hours when, with God's help, I will forever end this man's reign of terror.' Here the film administers the first of what will be several reversals, moments when our understanding of a particular situation is suddenly revealed as hopelessly inadequate. All along we, the audience, had assumed from our prior knowledge of vampire films that Harker was the unsuspecting innocent, and Hammer had encouraged us in this by making Harker's first diary entry deliberately ambiguous and by rendering Harker himself something of a blank slate, reacting only minimally to the events going on around him. But now, in what is a spectacular departure from Stoker's novel and all stage and film adaptations, we see that this was a performance, that just as Dracula is pretending to be the perfect host, so Harker is pretending to be the perfect guest. Librarianship is simply a cover, for he is in actuality a vampire hunter with the requisite knowledge to destroy the undead.[18] How effective a vampire hunter Harker will be remains to be seen, although already there are signs that he is not sufficiently authoritative to take on this particular vampire. In part this comes from John Van Eyssen's rather diffident performance in the role, but it is also to do with the character's lack of curiosity (he does not even try to explore the castle when he has the opportunity) and the fact that twice he has been taken by surprise and his vision revealed as ineffective – the first time when the female vampire appears behind him, the second with Dracula's appearance on the stairs.

The scene that follows establishes fairly conclusively the worth of Jonathan Harker as hero. It relates loosely to a scene in the novel where Harker is 'seduced' by Dracula's three brides only to be rescued by Dracula himself, although, as before in the film, Hammer's treatment of this is very different. Harker falls asleep and is woken by the sound of his door being unlocked. Leaving his room, he makes his way into the library and into a scene that in certain respects is remarkably similar to the scene just concluded. In both, Harker encounters first the vampire woman and then Dracula, with on both occasions these two figures appearing suddenly and unexpectedly. The difference is that the decorous politeness of the earlier scene is, in the library, torn apart by acts of sexuality and violence, acts which, in the context of the repetition, seem as if they are erupting from within that initial decorum, revealing that which was previously hidden.

Again the woman appears from behind Harker and begs for his help. Eventually she moves closer to him and rests her head on his shoulder. There follows what even today, after a massive proliferation of vampire fictions, is an electrifying moment. The woman slowly raises her head from Harker's shoulder, her mouth open enough for her fangs to be visible, and she bites Harker's neck. Here, for the first time ever in vampire cinema, the eroticism of the bite is unambiguously present, in the proximity of the bodies, in the intent expression on the woman's face, in the physicality of the bite itself. This physicality is carried over into the remainder of the scene. As Harker recoils, there is a shock cut to Dracula standing in the open doorway, snarling, with blood running from his mouth. No longer the polite host, he leaps over a table, grabs the woman and throws her across the room. Harker intervenes only to be half-choked and thrown across the room in the opposite direction, from which position he watches helplessly as Dracula carries his now unconscious 'bride' away. At this point Harker passes out.

Previous film vampires had rarely touched their victims, preferring to mesmerise them and then bite them offscreen. Here, by contrast, we are shown the bite in close-up, and the strength of the vampire is also portrayed in the most direct way. The sight of Dracula and the woman hissing animalistically at each other speaks in this respect of a physical sexual energy, the likes of which had rarely been seen either in earlier horror films or in British cinema.[19] By the end of the sequence, the truth is out: the woman is a vampire, Dracula is strong, and Harker, for all his knowledge and preparedness, is weak, not just in comparison with Dracula but also in relation to the woman he allowed to bite him. The fact that Harker was forewarned of the danger in the castle merely accentuates this weakness and, in line with this, the remainder of this part of the film traces the complete collapse of any authority he might once have had.

When Harker recovers consciousness, he finds himself back in the room where he awoke in the previous scene (another of the film's many repetitions). In the absence of any evidence to the contrary, one has to assume that he was carried from the library by Dracula in exactly the same way that the vampire woman was carried from the library. Underlining this 'feminine' weakness, Harker's final diary entry acknowledges the possibility of defeat. He notes that he has been bitten and possibly infected by a vampire. 'It may be that I am doomed to be one of them. If that is so, I can only pray that whoever finds my body will possess the knowledge to do what is necessary to release my soul.' Having written this, Harker briefly leaves the castle and deposits his diary at a crossroads before making his way to the cellar.

The scene that follows builds further on the repetitions already introduced in the library scene. For the third time, Harker encounters two vampires, first the vampire woman and subsequently Dracula, although what was all-round politeness in the beginning and sexuality and violence in the library has here finally become a matter of life and death.[20] Given the prominence of Dracula's tomb in the cellar, and the fact that Harker looks into it from the top of the stairs by which he enters, it is all the more striking that this supposedly knowledgeable vampire hunter heads directly for the less dangerous female's tomb. Could this be Harker's revenge on the vampire that has infected him? If so, it is a rather foolish and petulant gesture from someone who should know better. Harker places the wooden stake upon the sleeping woman's chest and with the other hand raises a mallet. The film then cuts to Harker's shadow as the mallet comes down upon the stake. In its reliance on shadow, this shot seems to refer back very directly to the German Expressionist horrors of such films as *The Cabinet of Dr Caligari* (1919) and *Nosferatu* (1922). In itself, it is not at all typical of Hammer's more solidly realist style. However, when one considers the sound that accompanies this image, the distinctive Hammer style becomes more apparent. The sound of the mallet hitting the stake and the sound of the woman's scream both stand in for and themselves represent the physicality of the staking, an act which because of censorship constraints could not have been represented directly in any event.

Another significant element is introduced at the moment of the staking itself via a cut to a close-up of Dracula in his coffin as his eyes open. There is an anxious expression on his face as he hears the sound of his bride's death but then, with Harker still standing over the body of the now horribly aged woman, night suddenly falls – and Dracula smiles. The fact that at this crucial moment the Count is unable to see what is happening elsewhere in the cellar to his 'bride' underlines the way in which this whole scene, which marks the culmination of Harker's adventures at Castle Dracula, is organised around a restriction of vision. We (and, for that matter, Dracula) know that the woman has been staked only because we hear it. We (and Dracula) do not see her transformation into an aged hag. We (and Dracula) do not directly see night falling but only glimpse it through a stained-glass window. We are not aware that Dracula has left his tomb until Harker himself realises that the tomb is empty. And, finally, when Dracula appears to Harker – re-enacting his first appearance by standing at the head of a flight of stairs – we do not see what the Count does to Harker for, as Dracula closes the cellar door, the film fades ominously to black.

The elliptical nature of the scene makes it an appropriate climax to Harker's story which, as noted above, has already had more than its share of ambiguities. The scene might also be viewed as an elaboration of the moment in the titles sequence where the camera tracks towards Dracula's tomb only to be confronted with an ambiguous image of bloodshed. In each case, the camera becomes the site of a failed vision – Harker's vision, our vision – and an associated failure of action. This is Dracula's world, the film seems to say, a world in which nothing is what it seems – not Dracula, not his vampire consort, not even Harker himself.

Even as it does this, the cellar scene also sets up certain parameters so far as the vampire, or rather the Hammer vampire, is concerned. For all his power, Dracula is given us, albeit briefly, as a vulnerable figure, lying prone in his tomb, presumably in suspense as to whether Harker will get to him before night falls. That the coming of night turns out to be instantaneous, with no interim twilight period, is also significant in this respect, for the suddenness of the change relates to, and in a sense is itself an expression of, other rapid changes going on in the scene – night falls instantly, Dracula instantly moves from a position of weakness to one of power, the woman changes instantly from youthful beauty to old age.[21] I have already noted the importance to the film of notions of transformation and energy, and here, in the final part of Harker's story, the film-makers have orchestrated multiple transformations in an especially dynamic way, with Dracula fully caught up in this process. Christopher Lee has identified certain features of Stoker's Dracula that were important to him in his performance in Hammer's film: 'his extraordinary stillness, punctuated by bouts of manic energy with feats of strength belying his appearance'.[22] This counterpointing of stillness and energetic outbursts can be seen to characterise not only Lee's Dracula but also the opening twenty minutes of the film as we are moved back and forth between sequences of decorous politeness and scenes of frantic violence.

The comprehensive failure of Harker to defeat Dracula is an unexpected turn in the narrative. John Van Eyssen is clearly not the star of the film, so the dispensing of a main character relatively early on in the film is not as shocking as it would be two years later in Hitchcock's *Psycho*. However, the conclusion of this part of *Dracula* does leave an audience wondering how the film will proceed. Regardless of the break in the narrative introduced by Harker's defeat, however, the first part of the film has introduced and developed elements that will be significant later on. In particular, the sequence's reliance on repetition-in-difference is one that will inform the film as a whole. A pattern has already become apparent by which the Harker–Dracula–vampire woman triangle is assembled three times, with each of these assemblages more sexual and violent than its predecessor. The differences between these encounters, differences to do with location and the stripping away of decorum, are clarified and accentuated by the sense that we are returning here to a particular dramatic situation again and again, probing deeper each time. This process does not finish with Harker's defeat but will continue throughout the Hammer *Dracula*, and in large part it is this sense of repetition, of constantly returning to particular dramatic configurations, that gives the film its dramatic weight and density.

The other important feature introduced in the sequence is, of course, Count Dracula himself. This chapter has already discussed some of the techniques used by the film-makers to represent the vampire, but something should also be said about his 'lifestyle'. This Dracula lives in a well-kept house rather than in a ruined castle, and he only has one 'wife' as opposed to Lugosi's (and Stoker's) more scandalous three; and they sleep, respectfully, in separate tombs, with the woman's tomb located deferentially at the foot of the resting place of her 'husband'. In this respect Dracula's fight with his female companion in the library starts to look like a domestic dispute between husband and wife into which an increasingly child-like and ineffectual Harker has unwittingly wandered. As will soon become apparent, the Hammer Dracula is also not the geographically distant figure embodied in both Stoker's and Lugosi's Dracula but instead someone who lives a mere horse-ride away from the city where much of the rest of the film will take place. In short, this Dracula, while still very much an aristocrat, is also one of the more bourgeois of cinema's vampires and not entirely dissimilar from the characters upon whom he will prey, and some of the implications of this changed relationship between Dracula and the forces of normality are about to be played out.

VAN HELSING'S STRENGTH

In Stoker's *Dracula*, Van Helsing, the vampire's nemesis, does not arrive at Castle Dracula until near the end of the narrative. In the 1931 Universal-Lugosi *Dracula*, he does not get to Transylvania at all (although

5. *Dracula (Christopher Lee) and Mina (Melissa Stribling) in a publicity still for Dracula.*

he does finally arrive there in the 1936 sequel, *Dracula's Daughter*). In the Hammer version, Van Helsing shows up in Transylvania immediately after the Harker section of the film has concluded. In part, this early entrance reflects the film's different regime of belief, notably the way in which it offers a world that has little time for disbelief in vampires and where consequently Van Helsing himself is a much more central and acceptable figure than he is in Stoker's novel. In other respects, this section of the film – which details Van Helsing's arrival at an inn and his subsequent exploration of Castle Dracula – stands in distinct contrast to the preceding Harker section, offering an implicit comparison between the weak Harker and the more authoritative Van Helsing. It is only a short sequence, seven minutes in comparison with the twenty minutes of the Harker sequence, but it marks an important turning point in the narrative.

The sequence begins with a brief establishing shot of a country inn and then cuts inside to show us garlic attached to the ceiling. Interestingly, the film-makers seem to assume here that, first, an audience will know what garlic looks like (which, in the context of Britain in the late 1950s, is quite a daring assumption), and that, second, it will know that vampires are allergic to garlic. In a later sequence, Van Helsing will spell out in detail what harms a vampire (including garlic); here, by contrast, no such explanation is forthcoming, and the presence of the garlic, and Van Helsing's knowledgeable response to it, serves mainly to establish the fearful superstition of the peasants who occupy the inn.

These peasants look up at the sound of a door opening. There is a cut to the person who has just entered. He is filmed from behind as he advances through the inn towards the landlord. As the camera starts to retreat, we finally see that the inn's new customer is Peter Cushing (although he will not be identified as Van Helsing for a few more minutes). It was Cushing, rather than the relatively unknown Christopher Lee, who was the film's top-billed star, and of all the actors in the film the one most recognisable to audiences, to international audiences through his performance in *The Curse of Frankenstein* and to British audiences through his many starring appearances on British television throughout the 1950s.[23] The withholding from us of Cushing's face until he speaks to the landlord is, then, the customary build-up to the star's entrance, as opposed to Lee's entrance which is more about introducing a character (although, of course, in later *Dracula* films, Lee himself would take on the role of star). However, Van Helsing's and Dracula's first appearances do have something in common, namely their reliance on an audience's restricted vision: we do not see Dracula enter, he is just there; similarly, we do not see Van Helsing enter the inn but instead see the reaction of others to his presence. Later in the film, parallels between Van Helsing and Dracula will be developed at some length with particular reference to their mastery of 'offscreen' space, but already here a sense of Van Helsing's controlling the space of the inn is being communicated via the way the camera follows him and then at a certain point backs away respectfully. One might compare this way of filming a character's movements with the more tentative, uncertain camerawork that accompanied Harker's earlier entrance into Castle Dracula.

The scene that follows involves Van Helsing quizzing the landlord and his female assistant about his friend, Jonathan Harker. 'He came here with a purpose, to help you,' he tells the landlord. 'We haven't asked for any help,' the surly landlord replies, only to be informed by Van Helsing, 'You need it all the same.' There is a rather obvious class dimension to this exchange, with Van Helsing as the middle-class 'gent' dominating this discussion with the peasantry. Hammer horror would never warm to the lower social orders and usually represented them as helpless victims of cruel aristocrats (see, for example, *The Hound of the Baskervilles*, *The Curse of the Werewolf* and *Plague of the Zombies* as well as, of course, *Dracula*) or as a mindless mob (e.g. *The Revenge of Frankenstein* and *The Gorgon*) or as just plain stupid (examples too numerous to mention). The superstitiousness of the peasants in *Dracula* clearly has a basis in what passes in the film for fact – i.e. vampires exist and they are repelled by garlic – but it is also a sign of primitive and child-like fears, something to be dispelled by the enlightened knowledge of a middle-class expert. Accordingly, it is Van Helsing who recognises the significance of the garlic in the inn and, like the equally middle-class Harker and in what might be seen as an equally patronising manner, has come to assist those incapable of assisting themselves.

'Some things are best left alone, such as interfering in things which are beyond our power,' grumbles the landlord, a line of dialogue that could easily have been left over from the earlier *The Curse of Frankenstein*. Van Helsing's reply is to the point: he does not scoff at the peasants' fears but instead implies that he understands the basis of those fears better than the peasants themselves: 'This is more than a superstition, I know. The danger is very real.' The body language of this exchange is as important in communicating its tone as what is actually being said. The landlord (played by portly Hammer regular, George Woodbridge) is physically uncomfortable in Van Helsing's presence; he very obviously wants the conversation to end, and ultimately issues a line that will be repeated later in the film by another character: 'I ask you to go and leave us in peace.' By contrast, Van Helsing is at ease but always watchful, attentive, perpetually ready. Van Helsing's persistence eventually pays off when the serving woman surreptitiously passes him Jonathan Harker's diary which, she tells Van Helsing, was found outside the castle (although by whom is never made clear). 'Your friend was such a nice gentleman,' she says of Harker, an appropriately deferential last line of dialogue for a scene that has established a certain authority for 'the gentleman' but which has also begun to distinguish Van Helsing from his hapless predecessor.

The next scene shows Van Helsing's arrival at the castle. As he does so, a hearse bearing a coffin is driven away. Having observed this, Van Helsing continues to follow in Harker's footsteps, first venturing into the castle and then upstairs into Harker's room. Here he finds a broken photograph frame with a small fragment of a photograph still in it. Given that we know that this was a photograph of Harker's fiancée, there is a hint here of where Dracula has gone, an intimation in fact of the vampire's limited aims in this film. Earlier film versions, and to a certain extent Stoker's novel as well, had been rather vague over the question of what Dracula actually wanted. His coming to England implied a kind of invasion, a seeking out of new blood that involved the proliferation of vampirism throughout English society. By contrast, Hammer's Dracula seems simply to be seeking a replacement for the female companion staked by Harker. The fact that he takes with him one coffin only, as opposed to the numerous boxes of earth taken by Stoker's Dracula, underlines the fact that he does not intend to be away from his comfortable home for long; and, as we will see, he is not travelling far in any event.

On arriving in the castle's cellar, Van Helsing, initially at least, does exactly what Harker did. He goes first of all to the woman's tomb and only then to the main tomb nearest the door. The difference is that the woman, now horribly aged, has already been staked, and that a befanged Jonathan Harker, rather than Dracula, lies in the main tomb. Van Helsing picks up the stake and mallet earlier dropped by Harker and he approaches Harker's prone body. Fade to black.

Two important issues arise from this moment. The first is a retrospective one: what exactly did Dracula do to Harker when he caught him in the cellar? Clearly he did not kill him, but did he bite him? According to Harker's own diary, he had already been infected by the female vampire, so Dracula did not need to bite Harker in order for him to become one of the undead. Given that the film has already firmly established the vampire's bite as an erotic act, the prospect of a male vampire biting or 'kissing' another male is one guaranteed to make all British film-makers of the late 1950s decidedly uneasy. Cultural historian Christopher Craft has noted of Stoker's *Dracula* that 'the sexual threat that this novel first evokes, manipulates, sustains, but never finally

represents is that Dracula will seduce, penetrate, drain another male...
Always postponed and never directly enacted, this desire finds evasive
fulfilment in an important series of heterosexual displacements.'[24] The
fade-to-black that occurs just as Dracula approaches Harker for the last
time can be seen in this respect as covering over an uncertainty on the
part of the film-makers as to what exactly happens next. Nevertheless,
Hammer's film goes further than Stoker's novel in offering us a male
vampire other than Dracula himself, although this is qualified by this
vampire's being glimpsed only briefly and when he is asleep.[25]

If this is such a potentially embarrassing moment for the film, one
has to consider why it was included. Why not have Dracula just kill
Harker and leave the corpse in his tomb as a warning to others? The
answer seems to have something to do with the way in which later in the
film Dracula will take Harker's place in the affections of Harker's fiancée.
Harker's being left as a vampire in Dracula's tomb signifies that the
weak Harker has in a sense 'become' Dracula, that the sexual force
embodied by the vampire comes from within the forces of normality
rather than from a distant alien location.[26]

The second issue arising from the conclusion of this part of the film
derives from the fact that it is Van Helsing who picks up the stake earlier
dropped by Harker and does something that Harker himself was unable
to do, namely destroy the vampire resting in Dracula's tomb. That the
vampire staked by Van Helsing turns out to be Harker himself merely
underlines something that has become increasingly apparent ever since
Van Helsing's entrance into the film, namely that while both these men
are middle-class vampire hunters, they are in important respects very
different from each other. Van Helsing's authoritative management of
the peasants has already been noted, and here he manages to complete
Harker's business in the cellar.

The nature of Van Helsing's authority merits some consideration.
Elsewhere I have argued, borrowing some terms from Michael Frayn,
that the Hammer film-makers of the 1950s and first part of the 1960s can
be viewed, so far as their values and the way in which they operated are
concerned, as Carnivores as opposed to the Herbivore film-makers
working at Ealing Studios during the 1950s.[27] Frayn used the terms
'Herbivore' and 'Carnivore' to describe what he saw as a change in
British national identity occurring around the time of the Festival of
Britain in 1951, in particular the supplanting of one form of middle-
class domination, the Herbivore form, by another, the Carnivore. For
Frayn, the Herbivores were 'the radical middle-classes – the do-gooders

... gentle ruminants ... who look out from the lush pastures which are their natural station in life with eyes full of sorrow for less fortunate creatures, guiltily conscious of their advantages, though not usually ceasing to eat the grass', while the up-and-coming Carnivores were 'the members of the upper- and middle-classes who believe that if God had not wished them to prey on all smaller and weaker creatures without scruple he would not have made them as they are'.[28] From this perspective, Harker is very much a Herbivore figure. He tries to help the peasants in his well-intentioned middle-class way but does not have the requisite ruthlessness to succeed. He clearly finds the whole business of staking vampires dreadfully traumatic and in the end is defeated by his own innate decency. Van Helsing is different inasmuch as he is a Carnivore, someone who leads because he has the inalienable right to lead. He might be on the side of goodness but in certain respects he is not dissimilar from that other arch-Carnivore, Count Dracula.

Hammer horror would always be remarkably intolerant of its Herbivore characters (just as Ealing in the post-war period would have little time for Carnivore beliefs), and *Dracula* is no exception. Van Helsing emerges from this as one of Hammer's savants, a middle-class male who is not only knowledgeable but also has the force of character to transform that knowledge into positive action, and in so doing to dominate others. It is the presence of characters of this type in a range of Hammer horrors that has enabled critics to identify these films as reactionary, as texts that promote essentially patriarchal and bourgeois values.[29]

It would be hard to argue that Hammer horror films are not in some way repositories of conservative, patriarchal and bourgeois values, but it can be reasonably argued, I think, that these films are ultimately more complex and ambiguous than this reading of them might suggest. This is already apparent in the way that Van Helsing has been presented to us in *Dracula*. Certainly he possesses a considerable authority, but this is ameliorated by the performance of Peter Cushing. Previous accounts of Hammer (and British cinema in general, for that matter) have not made much of the contribution of actors, but, in the case of *Dracula*, performance is crucial in helping to form a more nuanced treatment of ideas and values that at the script stage might have seemed rather schematic. Cushing's response to discovering that Harker has become a vampire is instructive in this respect. He briefly covers his face with one of his hands. Obviously he is stronger than Harker, who seemed traumatised after staking the female vampire, but the sadness and resignation on Van Helsing's face as he approaches the tomb make it clear that he is not simply the reactionary, stake-wielding fanatic that he is sometimes made out to be. Similarly, while his subsequent dealings with characters being threatened by Dracula often involve his asserting his own better understanding and issuing a series of commands, he never comes across as arrogant but instead as a concerned, humane man.

Of course, one might argue that such details in performance merely 'sugar the pill', so to speak: they make the character's essentially reactionary function more palatable without seriously challenging or problematising that function. It seems to me that such an approach, in its attempt to remove ambiguities in the interests of producing a neat, cohesive reading of the film, is in effect a denial of cinema's reliance on fascinating and ambiguous images, images that are designed to attract and hold an audience's attention without any particular regard for their ideological cohesion. I would argue that much of the pleasure and fascination of *Dracula* lies precisely in the details of its realisation – in its *mise-en-scène*, its use of sound, its performances – and that any meaningful account of it needs to be alert to the nuances of this realisation rather than simply trying to relate everything to a crude and one-dimensional moral-ideological framework. An important focus for nuance in the film is Cushing's performance. Most people now remember Lee's performance in *Dracula* as the central one; it is certainly a 'showstopper', and the actor's brooding presence was obviously a key element in the film's success. However, Cushing has arguably a more challenging part to play – he is on screen more often than Lee, has more dialogue, and he helps to set the tone of the proceedings to a greater degree. This chapter will later return to some of the details of this performance. At this stage of the film, it is probably enough to indicate that *Dracula* has successfully established a cinematic world in which some characters have authority – Dracula and Van Helsing – and other characters do not – Harker, the peasants. But this has not been presented schematically, and in certain ways the authority of both Dracula and Van Helsing has been shown as tentative, with Dracula's fear as he lies helpless in his tomb and Van Helsing's concern for his friend acting as important counterpoints to their undoubted power.

THE BATTLE FOR LUCY

After the eroticism and violence of Castle Dracula, we suddenly find ourselves in a decorous Victorian drawing room. Members of the audience familiar with Stoker's novel will no doubt assume that Hammer's film is simply replaying the transition made there from its wild Transylvanian setting to its more refined English ones; and, initially at least, the Hammer film-makers do nothing to upset this expectation. Only as this part of *Dracula* proceeds do we gradually start to notice that among the English character names are some German-sounding ones and that the city in which this drawing room is located seems to have German street names. Eventually we discover that this city is called Carlstadt and it is only a day's horse-ride from Castle Dracula. Paradoxically perhaps, the first English vampire film is not actually set in England.

This change of location from the novel seems to have been made without much concern for the incongruity of having predominantly English characters within an apparently German, Austrian or Swiss setting, and no concern whatsoever for geographical accuracy. A quick glance at a map of Europe will confirm that the fastest horse in the world could not travel from a German-speaking country to Transylvania in the space of one night as appears to happen at the end of Hammer's *Dracula*. Of course, this presupposes that Dracula's castle is located in Transylvania. I have assumed that here because it is so much a convention of *Dracula* adaptations. Yet the nearby village in Hammer's version is called Clausenberg, hardly a Romanian-sounding name, and Transylvania is never mentioned in the film's dialogue. In the climactic chase that concludes the film, a national border is crossed on the way back to Castle Dracula but it is not at all clear what border this is.[30] This is just one part of a more general vagueness in the film's construction of space, both in terms of where particular locations are in relation to other locations and in terms of the internal geography of some of the individual sets.

One can easily use this spatial 'messiness' as a stick with which to beat the film, and Hammer horror in general. How careless these film-makers are, and how contemptuous of their audience to assume that it would not notice these 'mistakes' (and how stupid of the audience for not actually noticing them and instead making the film a huge commercial success). It cannot be denied: as a geography lesson, *Dracula* is an abject failure. Put as bluntly as this, it should be clear how misguided such a critique of the film actually is, how it misses the point in a very fundamental way. *Dracula*, after all, is a low-budget fantasy film, and the way in which it was made is informed by both the budgetary and the fantasy elements.

The low budget has led to a compression of space that reflects the restricted space of the tiny Bray Studio in which the film was produced.

So Castle Dracula is relatively small and we do not get to see much either of it or of the Holmwood house that is the main setting for the second half of the film. The lengthy sea-and-land journey between England and Transylvania that was so important in Stoker's novel has, in part, been removed for similar budgetary reasons (as was the case with the 1920s stage version of *Dracula*). But the space of the film is also an imaginative fantasy space, one that is not fully bound by notions of the real. So far as the film's broader geography is concerned, the closeness of the castle to the Holmwood house serves, as already indicated, a thematic function – Dracula is 'closer to home' than ever before. It also has a dramatic function relating to the pacing of the narrative. As we shall see, the narrative moves at increasing speed as it progresses, and by the time we get to the final ride to the castle, the imperative is to make this as rapid and breakneck as possible. Any lengthy journey would here impede the sprint to closure that organises the film's final section. It is interesting to compare this with what is often seen as the anti-climactic narrative trajectory of Stoker's novel, which concludes with a long, slow journey back to the castle and a rather half-hearted destruction of the Count.

Within such a stripped-down and focused context, what is not deemed important to the progression of the narrative gets pushed to one side. Fundamentally, place-names and geographical locations do not matter in the film, hence their rather cursory treatment (any name will do, it seems, so long as it sounds vaguely 'continental'). What matters is the dramatic relationship between these elements, and here the film-makers do the utmost within the limited resources available to them to create something distinctive. In effect, what the Hammer team does in *Dracula* – and more successfully than in its previous Gothic, *The Curse of Frankenstein* – is conjure up a world that, for all its solid physicality, stands apart from quotidian notions of the real, that in certain respects has a magical character.

Not that one would think this from the opening scene of the Carlstadt part of the film, which, in comparison with the movement and emotion of the previous scenes, is restrained to the point of stasis. Van Helsing, up until now so mobile, sits motionless in a chair, his hands placed neatly on his knees, while Arthur, standing, quizzes him about Harker's mysterious death and a seated and mostly silent Mina looks on. An absence of camera movement enhances the theatrical, tableau-like quality of the scene. Interestingly, Van Helsing makes no attempt to inform Arthur and Mina of what really happened to Jonathan. In this picture

of domestic 'normality', the first in the film, he clearly sees his task as
to protect this couple from the truth and to protect normal life in general
from a contaminating knowledge of the vampire.

It is worth mentioning here the changes wrought by Hammer on
some of Stoker's original characters. Already noted has been Harker's
transformation from an unsuspecting innocent into a knowledgeable
vampire hunter. Van Helsing and Dracula too are different: in Stoker's
novel, both are foreign, with Van Helsing speaking a bizarre form of
broken English, but in Hammer's film they sport impeccable English
accents. Hammer's versions of Arthur and Mina also turn out to be
different from their literary originals. The novel's Arthur is Arthur
Holmwood, Lord Godalming, who in the course of the narrative becomes the fiancé of Lucy Westernra; the film's Arthur is not a Lord but
instead the middle-class Arthur Holmwood. Mina, who in the novel
becomes Harker's wife, is here married to Arthur, while the yet-to-be-
seen Lucy is not Lucy Westernra (the surname means 'light of the west'
– a good example of Stoker's rather crude symbolism) but rather Lucy
Holmwood, Arthur's sister and Harker's fiancée. As for the other members of Stoker's 'Crew of Light', Harker is already dead, the Texan
Quincey Morris does not appear at all, and Dr Seward has been reduced
to a minor walk-on part.

The shifting round of characters and character names is commonplace in *Dracula* adaptations, and the particular configuration offered by
each version often provides a key to understanding that version's
approach to the *Dracula* story. In the case of Hammer's version, the
reworking of the characters' interrelationships produces a scenario in
which all of the main characters – with the notable exception of Van
Helsing and Dracula – are related either by blood or marriage (or
engagement) to the Holmwood family. It follows that there are only two
significant locations in the film: Arthur's house and Dracula's house. At
first they seem antithetically opposed, with Arthur's house standing for
all that is normal and Dracula's house for evil and deviancy. However,
given that Dracula's house has already been presented in certain respects
as a domestic location where a paterfamilias dominates his woman, certain
parallels with Arthur's house quickly become apparent. Like Dracula,
Arthur is clearly the 'lord' of his house, with his wife sitting submissively
in his presence; and like Dracula and his 'bride', Arthur and Mina do not
have children in 'the accepted sense of the term' (to borrow a phrase
from *Dracula – Prince of Darkness*) but instead treat the daughter of their
housekeeper as if she is their own. As the first scene of this part of the

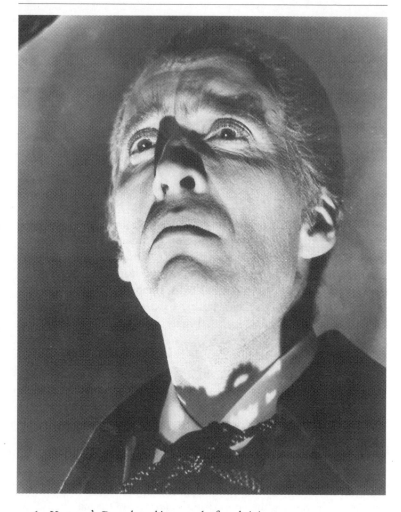

6. *Hammer's Dracula at his most aloof and sinister.*

film concludes, this sense of a resemblance between Arthur's and Dracula's homes is about to become yet more apparent.

On Van Helsing's departure, Arthur and Mina go to Lucy's room. As Lucy is ill and confined to her bed, they decide not to tell her about Jonathan's death, protecting her just as Van Helsing protected them from the truth about Jonathan. Lucy seems devoted to Harker and quite unlike the flighty Lucy in Stoker's novel whose scandalous independence, it has been suggested by critics, leaves her open to vampiric infection. This

Lucy lies passively in bed, looking delicate and pretty in her blue night-dress and waiting for her Jonathan to return. Like Mina, she is the 'good' woman where goodness involves a deference to male authority – a world away, it seems, from the other woman in the film, the predatory female vampire who assaulted Harker (although, of course, even that female is made to defer to Dracula). However, something said by Mina during the bedroom scene does give a hint that all is not well. Noting Lucy's paleness, Mina comments, 'You've got to get some colour back into those cheeks.' For anyone even remotely familiar with the conventions of vampire films, a comment of this kind betokens certain doom for the character to whom it is addressed. In confirmation of this, a startling transformation occurs in Lucy the moment she is alone. As sinister music is heard on the soundtrack, she suddenly becomes animated, getting out of bed, opening the french windows, removing the cross from around her neck and then arranging herself on the bed. She looks longingly at the open window, and any doubt still in our mind about her having already fallen under Dracula's influence is quickly removed by the sight of the two puncture wounds on her neck.

As is so often the case in the Hammer *Dracula*, this moment both replays and reworks images and events from earlier in the film. The transformation of Lucy from helpless passivity to eroticised activity is comparable with the vampire woman's change from being Dracula's 'prisoner' to being the woman who sinks her fangs into Harker's neck. Both instances rely on notions of female performance, of women pre-tending to be something they are not. David Pirie has noted that 'one of the more appalling things that Dracula does to the matronly women of his Victorian enemies (in the novel as in the film) is to make them sensual'.[31] One might add to this, in regard to Hammer's *Dracula* in particular, that the Count also bestows on these woman an ability to dissimulate, to play the role of 'the good woman', with these deceptive performances directed primarily at men.

Lucy's transformation in Hammer's *Dracula* comprehensively under-mines the picture of normality with which we had been presented in only the previous scene. Arthur might believe that all is well in his house, but, as with Dracula's house, appearances are deceptive. What Arthur sees is his sister lying meekly in bed; the moment his back is turned, not just his sister but his sister's room changes. As the lights are switched off, the room is bathed in a blue light. It is as if the pretty blue of Lucy's nightdress has suddenly become sinister and expansive, an expression of a previously repressed sexuality. Throughout the film, blue will be Lucy's colour; her later appearance as a vampire will be filmed in a blue-tinged light and only after she has been staked by Van Helsing will she be lit in a more conventional manner.

As Lucy waits expectantly for her vampire lover, there is a cut to Van Helsing in his study reciting facts about vampires into a recording machine. In Stoker's novel, a machine of this kind features as one of the numerous signifiers of modernity associated with the vampire hunters. In Hammer's film the machine becomes instead a rather quaint part of the period setting, but it does afford Van Helsing the opportunity authoritatively to lay down the law about vampires. Here we are told about the vampire's susceptibility to light, garlic and the crucifix. We also learn that victims 'consciously detest being dominated by vampirism but are unable to relinquish the practice. Similar to addiction to drugs' (although whether Lucy looks like a drug addict while waiting for Dracula is another matter).

Cutting between Lucy's room and Van Helsing's study is clearly designed to set up a series of dramatic contrasts – between the feminine and the masculine, darkness and light, silence and speech, emotion and rationality. In essence, what this part of the film seems to be saying is that the male authority embodied in Van Helsing represents the solution to the 'problem' of Lucy. This presupposes a division between the powerful Van Helsing and Arthur Holmwood who, it appears, is master of his house in name only. But there is also an undercurrent of unease here. Lucy looks at the window for her lover and the next thing we are shown is Van Helsing. Then, at the end of the Van Helsing scene, there is a sudden cut to Dracula at Lucy's window, standing in the same place compositionally as Van Helsing in the previous shot. There is a strong sense here, pictorially and in terms of our perceptions of these characters, that these two men are in certain respects similar. They are both men of power and authority who stand apart from the other men in the film. These are well-matched adversaries, we feel, although they will not actually meet until near the end of the film. In the meantime their ongoing struggle will be carried out through the bodies of two women – first Lucy and then Mina.

The film then proceeds quickly to Lucy's death. We see Lucy's doctor, Dr Seward, express to Mina his bafflement over her case. Mina then decides to involve Van Helsing. She visits him and gives information about Lucy's symptoms. At first, Van Helsing does not seem that interested, but when Mina remarks that the doctor thinks Lucy's condition to be anaemic, his expression changes. In fact, he reacts in a way that he will react at later key points in the film, moving instantly to a position of alertness and readiness. These transformations, involving the body tensing and an intent expression appearing on his face, are always in response to events or communications that have little significance for the other characters in the film. Thus not only Van Helsing's superior knowledge but also his disciplined ability to act effectively on that knowledge manifest themselves. In this case, Mina does not realise the importance of her own words, but Van Helsing does and immediately he takes charge of the situation. He visits Lucy and sees the wounds on her neck. Again there is an instant reaction – he knows exactly what these wounds mean – but again he chooses not to share his knowledge with anyone else. Instead he issues a series of orders: keep the window shut, fill the room with garlic, etc. 'If you love Miss Lucy, be guided by me, I beg you,' he tells Mina, and then, yet more firmly, 'I cannot impress upon you strongly enough how important it is that you obey my instructions. Do exactly as I say and we may be able to save her.' Needless to say, Van Helsing's orders are not followed to the letter. The garlic is removed from Lucy's room and the window opened by Gerda, the gullible and foolish housekeeper (yet another of Hammer's unflattering portrayals of the working class), and consequently Lucy dies.

An odd feature of the scenes depicting Van Helsing's involvement in the Lucy Holmwood case is the absence from them of Arthur Holmwood. Given that Lucy is his sister, one would have thought that he would have been party to the decision to invite Van Helsing back to the house, but there is no indication of this. One assumes that this is for reasons of dramatic convenience; Arthur had already made it clear that he was not satisfied by Van Helsing's explanation of Harker's death, and it is unlikely that he would have welcomed Van Helsing's further involvement in their lives. Arthur's resistance to Van Helsing is about to become the focus of the narrative but as it would needlessly have slowed down the events leading up to his sister's death, the film temporarily removes him. Even as it does this, however, it also presents us with a situation that we have seen before, one in which a woman goes behind a man's back in order to help Van Helsing. The first time it was the woman in the inn who, disobeying the innkeeper, passed Harker's diary to Van Helsing; here it is Mina, acting apparently without consulting Arthur, who involves Van Helsing. If this sounds a rather fanciful and forced comparison, it is worth considering a remark made by Arthur to Van Helsing as they stand by Lucy's deathbed. 'Please go and leave us in peace,' he says, offering a near verbatim repeat of the innkeeper's earlier

'I ask you to go and leave us in peace'. Despite their class differences, it seems that these two men have something in common – namely, a 'closed' view of the world and an inability to control their women.

The story of the pricking of Arthur's pomposity is as rapid and compressed as all the other dramatic transformations in the film. In the scene immediately following that in which he asks Van Helsing to leave, Tania, the housekeeper's daughter, informs him that she has seen Lucy alive. In the next scene after that, we find Arthur in the graveyard discovering that Lucy's tomb is empty. The film cuts away briefly to show Lucy meeting Tania and then returns to the graveyard, a splendidly atmospheric location thanks to Bernard Robinson's design and Jack Asher's lighting, for the meeting between Arthur and Lucy. In what is becoming a familiar pattern for the film, what follows both refers back to and elaborates upon earlier events. Lucy's movement towards her brother through the graveyard restages her movement through the bedroom as she prepares herself for Dracula. In each, a figure in blueish-white moves aggressively towards the camera. The key difference here, aside from the fact that Lucy is now a vampire, is that at the end of the movement in the bedroom scene Lucy removes the cross from around her neck, while in the graveyard scene, as if in response to this earlier action, a crucifix is thrust into her face and the shape of the cross is burned on to her forehead. The change that occurs in Lucy when confronted with the crucifix – from temptress to snarling, animalistic vampire – is as instantaneous as all the other transformations we have seen thus far in the film: in Hammer's *Dracula*, nothing ever happens slowly. In line with this, the appearance of the crucifix itself is sudden and unexpected, and it involves a 'magical' control over offscreen space that we have come to associate with Dracula, although here it is Van Helsing who, apparently appearing from nowhere, intervenes between brother and sister.

The cessation of Lucy's mobility leads logically enough to her staking. There are two distinct ways of thinking about what happens to Lucy. The reading offered very explicitly both by Hammer's film and Stoker's novel is that her destruction represents the triumph of good over evil. The other reading, associated primarily with feminist critics, involves seeing Lucy's staking as a coded act of male violence directed against a rebellious female; the stake is endowed here with a phallic quality and the staking itself becomes a kind of symbolic rape. Certainly, to modern eyes at least, the novel's account of this event does lend itself more to the latter reading than it does to the former:

The Thing in the coffin writhed; and a hideous, blood-curdling screech came from the opened red lips. The body shook and quivered and twisted in wild contortions; the sharp white teeth champed together till the lips were cut, and the mouth was smeared with a crimson foam. But Arthur never faltered. He looked like a figure of Thor as his untrembling arm rose and fell, driving deeper and deeper the mercy-bearing stake, whilst the blood from the pierced heart welled and spurted up around it. His face was set, and high duty seemed to shine through it; the sight of it gave us courage, so that our voices seemed to ring through the little vault.[32]

There is something vaguely pornographic here, not just in the excitability of the language but also in the writhing of Lucy's body as it is penetrated by the 'mercy-bearing' stake wielded by the upright (erect?) Thor-like Arthur.

Whether or not one accepts such a reading of Lucy's destruction in Stoker's novels (and most *Dracula* critics do broadly subscribe to it), it does not necessarily follow, however, that Lucy's staking in subsequent adaptations is bound to have the same significance. It certainly should not be assumed, as some critics seem to assume, that whenever a female vampire is staked by a male vampire hunter the stake is automatically and invariably phallic, and the act itself always a sexual one. Instead one needs to attend to the dramatic contexts within which such acts occur and in relation to which they acquire their significance for audiences.

The staking of Lucy in Hammer's *Dracula* is different from the depiction of the event in Stoker's novel in several important ways. For one thing, it is Van Helsing who administers the stake rather than Arthur (and, as already noted, Arthur here is not Lucy's aristocratic fiancé but instead her brother). For another, there is none of the quasi-sexual writhing of the vampire's body described by Stoker, just a scream as the stake is hammered home offscreen. In Stoker's novel, Arthur's action is clearly meant to be seen as heroic; in Hammer's version, by contrast, there is much less stress on heroism. Instead the scene is filmed in such a way that it reminds us of Van Helsing's earlier staking of Harker. In each case, the staking is offered – both through Cushing's performance and through a reticence about showing details of the staking itself – as something that is unpleasant but necessary. Accordingly, once he has staked Lucy, Hammer's Van Helsing makes Arthur look at her body in order that he may see her restored to 'peace' and understand the reason for the staking; in a sense, the education of Arthur is as important here as what has happened to his sister.[33]

Is Van Helsing's staking of Lucy in the Hammer *Dracula* a symbolic rape designed to put her back in her place and restore the male authority that she had threatened? I would argue that this is much too crude a reading of what is going on in this part of the film. It is not just that Van Helsing turns out to be an 'equal opportunities' staker who approaches the staking of male and female vampires in a similarly professional and dedicated manner. It is also that Lucy never really threatens Van Helsing's authority, only the authority of her brother; and, as we have seen, Arthur is not a particularly authoritative or attractive figure in the first place. Indeed, it is his body that does the writhing in Hammer's version of the staking as he seems to identify with his sister at the moment of her destruction. In effect, what the staking achieves is not the restoration of authority but rather the delivery of Arthur into the hands of Van Helsing, for whom he will become a willing and devoted helper. Seen in this way, the staking scene speaks as much of male weakness, Arthur's weakness, as it does of male power, Van Helsing's power; and it is one of the film's more interesting features that it is never able to put together into a cohesive whole these two images of masculinity.

As for poor Lucy, her challenge to male definitions of her role turns out to be a very modest one. In part, this is to do with the speed of the film's narrative; she is already 'infected' when we first see her, and within only a few minutes she is dead, resurrected and then staked. One could reasonably argue that the marginalisation of Lucy that this involves is simply another form of coded violence against women, this time the violence of exclusion; and certainly the Hammer *Dracula*, even by the standards of *Dracula* adaptations generally, is male-centred. But if Hammer's *Dracula* is a repository of patriarchal values, it is so in its own distinctive way, and understanding how it actually operates is not best served by lumping it in with all the other *Dracula* stories as a rather monolithic expression of male fears about female sexuality.

THE BATTLE FOR MINA

Just before he stakes Lucy, Van Helsing raises with Arthur the possibility of using her to help track down Dracula. Arthur is appalled. 'How can you suggest such a thing?' he asks, and Van Helsing, sensitive to his feelings, drops the idea. Thus Lucy's death, like the death earlier of Harker, acts as a kind of pause in the narrative. Dracula himself has appeared only once in the 'Lucy' section of the film, and his whereabouts remain unknown. In the immediate post-staking scene, one thing has changed, however. We find ourselves back in the Holmwood house, but instead of Arthur standing authoritatively over Van Helsing, as was the case at the start of the 'Lucy' section, this time it is Van Helsing who walks up and down as if he owns the house while Arthur is the seated one. 'I'll do anything you say,' Arthur tells Van Helsing, confirming his unquestioning acceptance of the older man's authority. Acceptance of this authority is not in itself enough, of course, as the fate of Jonathan Harker demonstrated. But so far as the film is concerned, it is a step in the right direction, and Arthur becomes a less pompous and more attractive character because of it.

The narrative then splits into two story-lines which are intercut with each other. One of these shows Van Helsing and Arthur in search of Dracula, visiting first a customs house and then an undertaker's where Dracula's coffin briefly resided. The other story-line depicts Mina being lured away from the Holmwood house and falling under Dracula's influence. On a certain level, this division relies on decidedly stereotypical notions of gender, with the heroic men setting out to save the day while the poor helpless woman falls victim to the enemy because the men are not there to protect her. However, perhaps surprisingly, the film undermines this in various ways. In part, this derives from the intercutting itself which juxtaposes male 'heroics' with the apparent failure of those heroics. It is also significant that both of Van Helsing and Arthur's encounters with officialdom are presented in comic terms. The scene with the wheezing, corrupt customs official is actually one of the clumsier episodes in the film and its 'humour' falls flat. The encounter with the undertaker, by contrast, is delightful thanks entirely to the performance of Miles Malleson. Malleson was a rotund, chinless character actor who appeared in numerous films from the 1930s onwards and in his later years did several comic cameos for Hammer horror. Terence Fisher, director of *Dracula*, once said that Malleson needed no direction at all and could make something entertaining out of nothing, and certainly the actor performs very ably in *Dracula* whereas the competent but uninspired actor playing the customs official struggles to make much of his unpromising dialogue. Regardless of the uneven quality of their execution, these two scenes stand out from a film that is predominantly sombre in tone. Later Hammer horrors would frequently feature such moments of 'comic relief' located on the margins of the narrative. Aside from the incidental pleasures they offer, their presence in *Dracula* seems to denote a temporary diminution in Van Helsing's effectiveness, presaging another reversal of fortune in the struggle with the vampire.

The other element that works against the idea of female helplessness is Mina herself. This is partly to do with casting. Lucy had been played by Carol Marsh, a gamine performer who spent most of her career playing ingenue roles in films like *Brighton Rock* (1947) and *Alice in Wonderland* (1950), while Mina is played by the apparently older and physically more imposing Melissa Stribling (although Stribling was actually only two years older than Marsh). To a certain extent, this reflects the novel's division between a flighty Lucy and the more sensible Mina, but in Hammer's *Dracula*, Mina's response to being 'vamped' is altogether different both from the virginal Lucy's fevered reaction and the literary Mina's intense disgust. As Mina arrives home after a night with Dracula, she finds an unsuspecting Arthur waiting for her. There is an enigmatic smile on her face, a smile which clearly indicates sexual pleasure but does so in the context of already existing sexual experience, hence Mina's calmness as opposed to the extremity of Lucy's response to Dracula.[34]

The men are thrown back on to the defensive once they realise that Mina is infected, and the 'defence of the house' scene commences. In this, Van Helsing and Arthur stand guard outside the house while Mina is supposedly safe inside. Unbeknown to the men outside, however, Dracula is already in the house vamping Mina. In fact the scene reiterates in a very focused and compressed way events that have gone before. Yet again the vampiric act is eroticised, with Mina in a nightdress and the biting taking place in the bedroom; yet again Dracula seems to have the ability to appear from nowhere; and yet again the film cuts between male heroics outside the house with the overcoming of those heroics inside the house. To all intents and purposes now, Arthur's house has become Dracula's house, and the defeat of the powers of normality seems complete. Things are about to change, however, and, this being Hammer's *Dracula*, the change will be sudden and extraordinarily energetic.

On their return to the house, Van Helsing and Arthur are dismayed to find Mina on the point of death. A transfusion scene ensues, with Arthur's blood pumped into Mina.[35] While resting downstairs, Arthur asks Gerda to get some wine. Gerda demurs, stating that Mina has told her on no account to go down to the cellar. A tired-looking Van Helsing lying back in an armchair is instantly transformed into alertness. As before, he understands the significance of the line before anyone else, including the person who delivers it. Without saying a word, he erupts (and I don't use the word lightly) out of his chair and runs out of the room. Cut to the cellar as Van Helsing enters and sees Dracula's elegant white coffin. He runs down the cellar steps to find that the coffin is empty. As he throws a crucifix into it, the cellar door opens again and Dracula enters. It is the first encounter in the film between Van Helsing and the vampire, and it lasts all of two seconds. Dracula hisses and leaves, locking the door behind him. Van Helsing spends the next few seconds banging on the door until Arthur, still none the wiser, lets him out. Before explanations can be offered, there is a scream from upstairs. An ever energetic Van Helsing runs across the hallway, vaults the stair banisters and hurries upstairs, followed at a more sedate pace by Arthur. There they find a hysterical Gerda who, after an authoritative slap from Van Helsing, informs them that Dracula has kidnapped Mina. The scene ends with Van Helsing and Arthur leaving the house in hot pursuit.

So far as narrative logic is concerned, it has to be admitted that this scene makes little or no sense. Dracula's hiding his coffin – the place where he rests helpless during daylight hours – in his enemy's house does seem an astonishingly foolhardy thing to do. And where is Dracula coming from when he returns to the cellar? Has he really just been wandering aimlessly through the Holmwood house, somehow escaping detection? And, most of all, there is the question of the scene's time-frame. Van Helsing and Arthur enter the house at or near dawn. The transfusion follows, they go downstairs, and then Gerda issues the line about the cellar that alerts Van Helsing to Dracula's presence. Logically, this moment of discovery must occur during the daytime, and yet Dracula, who is allergic to sunlight, manages to leave the house with Mina a few seconds later, and the remainder of the film implies that the ride back to the castle, which takes place at night, follows on directly from Mina's abduction.

What the sequence lacks in narrative logic, however, it more than makes up for with a dynamism and energy. In fact, one might go further and suggest that the absence of logic helps the scene by freeing it from the need to explain methodically what is happening here and enabling it instead to proceed at speed. One can compare it in this respect with the film's rather shaky grasp of geography: what matters in the end is the dramatic use made by the film-makers of these various elements rather than their relation to more abstract notions of verisimilitude and plausibility. The scene of Dracula's discovery is organised around what can be termed here Van Helsing's will to action. His instant recognition of the significance of Gerda's line about the cellar produces an instant physical response, a blur of motion that both signals his power and marks a moment of reversal for Dracula who is immediately expelled

7. *Dracula (Christopher Lee) 'disciplines' his bride (Valerie Gaunt).*

from the Holmwood house. It is yet another of those sudden, violent transformations that have littered Hammer's *Dracula* and through which the battle between good and evil has largely been figured.

The chase is now on, and as Dracula, Mina, Van Helsing and Arthur all rush towards Castle Dracula, the film makes what is arguably its one misjudgement. This comes in the form of some dreadfully unfunny and inappropriate comic business at the customs house visited earlier by Van Helsing and Arthur. As both Dracula's and then Van Helsing's carriages crash through the flimsy wooden customs barrier, the customs official, dressed 'comically' in a nightshirt, emotes over-acted outrage. How one wishes for Miles Malleson here, although even he would probably have been out of place as the film draws to its frantic conclusion. Given that the rest of the film is so well-judged, one has to wonder why this scene was included. It might have had something to do with the need to build up what for a feature film was a relatively short running length (although this had not stopped the Hammer film-makers from cutting part of Harker's journey at the beginning of the film). It could also be seen as the film-makers' attempt at this point to separate the Holmwood house from Dracula's house. Ostensibly so different, there are moments in the film where they appear alarmingly similar: both domesticated settings ruled over by men, with in each case a coffin or tomb in the cellar. The customs house scene tries to establish a distance between the two houses, but it is unable to cover over the fact that what Dracula has done here is steal something that belongs to his 'neighbour' and is now hurrying home. Far from being the alien invader he is in Stoker's novel and to a certain extent in the 1931 Universal-Lugosi film, this Dracula emerges as someone whose major crime is a lack of respect for property rights. Accordingly, the first thing he does on arrival at his castle is start to bury Mina, not unlike a dog burying a bone. So much for the romantic but deadly lover.

Mina and Arthur are left behind at the castle entrance as Van Helsing pursues Dracula inside. There is more frantic motion, up staircases, into rooms, of the kind we have already seen in Arthur's house during Van Helsing and Dracula's first encounter. Eventually Van Helsing corners Dracula in the library and their final battle commences. There is none of the preliminary verbal jousting that one finds in the novel and other adaptations; in fact, this is perhaps the only version of *Dracula* where the Count and Van Helsing never speak to each other. Instead their fight is entirely physical as Van Helsing throws himself at Dracula and they wrestle across the library. Gradually the physically stronger Dracula gains the upper hand and, as Van Helsing backs away from him, all seems lost. All would be lost, in fact, if it were not for the final sudden reversal, one that is inaugurated by Van Helsing's glance at the curtained window. For all its brevity, the glance is crucial, for it signals that characteristic moment of thought that leads instantly into action. Van Helsing runs along the table and leaps off the end, pulling down the curtain with him. Light streams in through the window (clearly it is a typical Hammer day outside, with night instantly vanishing). Dracula seeks to escape but Van Helsing, using two candlesticks held up so they form an impromptu crucifix, forces him back into the light, and the vampire crumbles into dust.[36]

The scene's remarkable power has a lot to do with the physicality of the fight itself, a fight which in the context of its time is unprecedentedly violent and desperate. Earlier 'classic' fight scenes in British cinema – the fight between John Mills and Stewart Granger in *Waterloo Road* (1944) or the fight in the chapel in Hitchcock's *The Man Who Knew Too Much* (1934), for example – seem more polite, less raw in comparison. Of couse, this quality owes more than a little to the actors themselves. Both Lee and Cushing are extremely accomplished physical actors, and their movements and gestures bring a rhythm and a kind of beauty to the scene. One thinks here of the transformation from Lee's powerful stance, with claw-like hands spread out, to his contorted pose of subjection as he falls back into the light, and the juxtaposition of this with Cushing's more nervous performance style, full of expertly timed gestures expressing anxiety, intentness and pain. Hammer aficionados know that much of the business in this scene – the run along the table, using the candlesticks to form a crucifix – originated from Peter Cushing, always an active contributor to the films in which he appeared. (Sangster's original screenplay simply had Van Helsing using a crucifix to force Dracula into the light.) But the scene also benefits from cinematographer Jack Asher's lighting – the beam of light through the library window has an intensity that makes it easy for us to believe in its power – and from director Terence Fisher's compositions. Fisher's positioning of the long table and the beam of light at slanting angles both to each other and to the camera gives the scene, and the movements within it, a dynamic quality that, for all its action, it might otherwise have lacked.

I have already suggested that the film as a whole is organised around notions of power and powerlessness, with the relation between these two conditions constantly shifting. Some characters tend to be consistently powerless (Arthur Holmwood and Jonathan Harker) while others are more consistently powerful (notably Van Helsing and Dracula). But even the powerful ones undergo moments of subjection and vulnerability, none more so than Dracula and Van Helsing in the climactic fight. The whole scene depends on change, the change from night to day (reversing the day-to-night transition that sealed Harker's fate), Dracula's transformation into dust, and Van Helsing's own sudden transformation from potential victim to victor. It also depends on physical effort and an expenditure of energy from both characters, with the conclusion brought about, appropriately enough, by a pure beam of energy from the sun.

Critics have often seen Hammer horror films as reflecting a fixed morality whereby absolute good confronts and unambiguously defeats absolute evil. Such a reading seems inappropriate for the fight scene in *Dracula*, and indeed the film in which it appears, for here nothing is fixed; everything is in motion, everything unstable. The destruction of the vampire becomes in this respect not so much the triumphant victory of good over evil as it is a temporary suspension of activity in the dynamic, transformative world that has been conjured up by the Hammer *Dracula*.

CODA

As Arthur and Mina sit together outside Dracula's castle, the mark of the cross on Mina's hand that had signalled her possession by the vampire vanishes. Dracula is dead, and normality has been restored. This trajectory – whereby Dracula threatens to take Mina away and her husband (in the novel Harker rather than Arthur), with the help of others, wins her back – comes from Stoker's novel. There is a sense here of the woman as an object of exchange between men, an element stressed in the Hammer *Dracula* by Mina's muteness. Her last lines of dialogue were spoken when Arthur and Van Helsing discovered that she had fallen victim to Dracula. Since then, through the 'defending the house' scene and the climactic chase to the castle, she has not said a word, and she says nothing now as she is returned to her husband.

The film then cuts from this scene of connubial togetherness to Van Helsing inside the castle as he walks away from a window that presumably he has just opened. A breeze from outside blows Dracula's ashes across the floor, and the film ends. It says something about *Dracula*'s allegiances that it concludes in this way, not with the 'normal' couple but instead with the aftermath of the struggle between Van Helsing and Dracula, with Van Helsing himself visibly exhausted.

Throughout its length, Hammer's *Dracula* has presented a world characterised by sudden outbursts of energy and rapid metamorphoses, with this largely conveyed through the changeability of human bodies. In the previous scene, Dracula was himself transformed into ashes. Now the final image of the film – the ashes scattering in the breeze – indicates that this process of energetic transformation is not over, that this is still a world of movement and change. In comparison, the final image of

Arthur and Mina is a tokenistic gesture towards a conventional morality which the film subscribes to almost as a reflex action but which does not engage it in terms of the way it operates cinematically. What the film's true conclusion suggests – and it does this without knowledge of all the sequels to come – is that the intense relationship between control and subjection embodied in the conflict between Van Helsing and Dracula has not been finally resolved. It has sometimes been argued by horror historians that it is not until the late 1960s that the 'open' ending starts to become de rigueur for horror films. However, here in *Dracula* we already have a kind of open ending and a clear sense that, for all the drama of his destruction, Dracula will return.

THREE
The Mark of the Hammer *Dracula*

Dracula is a terrible film. *Dracula* is a wonderful film. *Dracula* degrades the concept of 'entertainment'. *Dracula* is a valuable example of British popular entertainment. *Dracula* is part of a vibrant Gothic tradition in British culture. *Dracula* gives Gothic a bad name. *Dracula* was directed by a talentless hack. *Dracula* was directed by a great British film-maker. *Dracula* is reactionary. *Dracula* is transgressive and radical. *Dracula* is a bad thing. *Dracula* is a good thing.

These are just some of the opinions and evaluations evident in the critical responses generated by the Hammer *Dracula* since its release in 1958. One way of dealing with and making sense of these responses is through contextualising them. It is certainly true that the critical reputation of *Dracula* has changed over the years, as the film moved from its initial disreputability to more positive evaluations and then, more recently, has come to be seen as a repository of conservative and patriarchal values. By relating various critical responses to the broader socio-historical and cultural contexts from which those responses emerged, one can gain a clearer sense of why the critics behaved in the way they did. Chapter One of this book has already pointed out that the history of the *Dracula* story is a history of constant reinterpretation; and much the same can be said for the Hammer *Dracula* as it is reinterpreted and revalued by different people within different contexts. In fact, the shifting critical fortunes of *Dracula* can be seen as an index of changes going on elsewhere, changes in attitude towards culture, British cinema and Britishness itself.

This chapter will explore what might be termed 'the legacy' of the Hammer *Dracula*. It will do this in part through looking at the original press responses to *Dracula* and subsequent critical reactions to the film, but it will also consider the responses of film-makers, those at Hammer and those working elsewhere, as these responses manifested themselves in other vampire films. As will become clear, *Dracula* exerted a considerable influence in both these areas, but it is also the case that the way in which this influence has operated has often obscured the significance of the Hammer *Dracula* itself.

THE CRITICAL RESPONSE

Like *The Curse of Frankenstein*, the Hammer *Dracula* received some decidedly mixed reviews on its initial release in May 1958. The most memorable of these tended to be the virulently negative ones. For example, Nina Hibbin, in the *Daily Worker*, offered the following:

> I went to see *Dracula*, a Hammer film, prepared to enjoy a nervous giggle. I was even ready to poke gentle fun at it. I came away revolted and outraged ... this film disgusts the mind and repels the senses ... Laughable nonsense? Not when it is filmed like this, with realism, and with the modern conveniences of colour and the wide screen ... This film is a degradation of cinema entertainment.[1]

An equally outraged C. A. Lejeune, noted film critic of the *Observer*, wrote:

> 'Don't dare see it alone!' is the adjuration printed in a black panel on the artistically blood-spattered synopsis of *Dracula*. For my own part, I wouldn't care to see the film with anybody else, preferring not to expose a companion to what seems to me a singularly repulsive piece of nonsense ... Will this wave of sensationalism die a natural death? Probably, but in the meantime it makes film-going a hazardous occupation.[2]

The extremity of such reviews, and their eminent quotability, has sometimes led to their being given undue weight and prominence in accounts of the way in which Hammer horror films were received in the late 1950s. Hammer historian David Pirie's suggestion that 'outraged critics fell over each other to condemn' *The Curse of Frankenstein* is slightly misleading in this respect, for in the case of both *The Curse of Frankenstein* and *Dracula* there were as many positive and indifferent reviews as there were negative ones.[3] The positive reviews of *Dracula* tended to focus on the film's production values. Particularly significant here were the trade papers which were less concerned with *Dracula*'s cultural status and more interested in its potential status in the marketplace. *Variety* praised the film's 'serious approach' and was impressed by 'producer Anthony Hinds' physical values and Bernard Robinson's art direction' while the *Daily Cinema* noted that 'Lavish settings and the magnificent use of backgrounds give the production a commanding appearance'.[4] Even some of the more negative reviews acknowledged that *Dracula* was well-made: for example, *The Star* noted that it was 'probably the best acted, directed and photographed horror film yet made'.[5]

With the benefit of hindsight, such reviews, and especially the extremely negative ones, can start to look rather quaint, with C. A. Lejeune's apology in her review to 'all decent Americans for sending them a work in such sickening bad taste' a particularly endearing example of a critical outrage that has dated badly. However, before dismissing these reviews out of hand and asserting our own more 'enlightened' appreciation of Hammer's *Dracula*, it is worth considering the context within which the original reviews, both the negative and the positive, were produced.

One element that preoccupied the reviewers of both *The Curse of Frankenstein* and *Dracula* was the X certificate awarded to both by the British Board of Film Classification (and which the advertising for each film exploited to the full). As noted in Chapter One, the X certificate had acquired an aura of disreputability during the 1950s, but by the time of Hammer horror, ABC and Rank, the two major British cinema circuits, were more willing to show such films as a way of arresting a decline in audience figures. In effect, the critics of *The Curse of Franken-stein* and *Dracula* were responding not just to the films but also to the changing nature of British cinema itself as it began to rely less on notions of 'family entertainment' and more on an often sensational type of film directed at the sixteen to twenty-four age range. For critics, the X certificate came to symbolise this change. '*Dracula* sounds the warning bell. One step farther and the licence permitted by the censor's X certificate will be dangerously abused,' writes one, while others preferred to suggest their own new certificates – with 'SO' for Sadists Only, 'S' for Sadistic, 'D' for Disgusting and 'M' for Moronic all cropping up in reviews of the late 1950s.[6]

One year after *Dracula*'s release, a film appeared that, according to the majority of British film critics, made the X certificate look like 'a badge of honour'.[7] The film was Jack Clayton's *Room at the Top*, a shocking (for the time) exposé of sexual mores in the North of England, which inaugurated a series of realist productions – among them *Saturday Night and Sunday Morning* (1960), *A Taste of Honey* (1961) and *A Kind of Loving* (1962) – that came to be known as the British New Wave.

These films were generally seen by critics at the time as introducing a welcome maturity into British cinema. The sense of the X certificate as a badge of honour, a marker of quality, was clearly meant to be contrasted, for the critics at least, with the exploitative, genre-based X-certificate cinema of which Hammer horror was part but which also included X-certificate crime thrillers and some of the less reputable social problem films.

The problem here for critics seemed not so much the genre films themselves as their popularity with audiences. In this respect, the success of films such as *The Curse of Frankenstein* and *Dracula* was seen as reflecting a degraded public taste, one which spoke of both a disturbed psychopathology and an impoverished cultural sensibility. For a discussion of the former, one can turn to 'The Face of Horror', a 'thought-piece' by Derek Hill that appeared in *Sight and Sound* in Winter 1958/59 and which linked horror's popularity with the anxieties of the nuclear age.

> The Bomb has obviously not caused the horror glut. But its existence has fostered an atmosphere in which the horror film has been able to develop in disturbing directions and on an unprecedented scale. The final analysis will find us a nation, probably a world, of quiet, controlled, largely unconscious hysterics, driven to that condition by submerged impotence and fear.[8]

For Hill, horror was clearly a symptom of a broader socio-psychological problem.

By contrast, the more populist publication *Films and Filming* offered two articles in the late 1950s that saw horror as part of the solution to psychological problems, as a kind of entertainment-therapy that helped an audience to come to terms with life's anxieties, Boris Karloff's 'My Life as a Monster' and Martin Grotjahn's 'Horror – Yes It Can Do You Good'.[9]

The other broader cause for concern addressed by reviews for early Hammer horrors involved the fear that cultural standards were being eroded by the introduction of an 'Americanised' mass culture into an increasingly affluent British society. One tangible expression of this concern had been the banning of American horror comics in Britain in 1955.[10] Another was Richard Hoggart's book *The Uses of Literacy*, published in 1957, which offered a powerfully negative view of the 'newer mass art' that was destroying traditional working-class culture. The fact that one of the British New Wave's major themes was a concern about the effects of consumerism upon social identities might in this respect help to explain its popularity with those critics who generally subscribed to the same set of anxieties about the changing state of Britain. So far as *Dracula* and other early Hammer horrors were concerned, the repeated description of them as 'degrading' reveals a concern about what this sort of 'exploitative' entertainment might be doing to an audience, how it might be blunting sensibilities and in so doing undermining class distinction (with this all made worse by the fact that these films were British rather than American). 'Horror. That's what we want more of. No class distinction in horror films – good for all types of halls,' a film booking agent is quoted as saying in a rather patrician article by Leonard Mosley, film critic of the *Daily Express*, an article entitled (apparently without any irony) 'The Audience is My Enemy'.[11] One has to assume that the audience here is the undiscriminating mass whose mere existence is an affront to more refined and implicitly middle-class aesthetic tastes.

Both as a symptom of a sick society and as an example of a degrading mass entertainment, *Dracula* represented for the critics of the late 1950s more than just a horror film, and they responded accordingly. From this perspective, the outraged reviews of a film that now seems relatively mild in terms of its representation of violence and sex start to make more sense. However, this should not stop us from judging the quality and validity of the readings of *Dracula* offered by its original critics. With this in mind, I want to focus on one review in particular, Peter John Dyer's in *Films and Filming*. While not as extreme or as outraged as some, the attitudes it displays are ones that inform many of the other reviews, both the negative and the positive. Because of this, it is worth quoting at some length.

> There are boring horror films and tasteless horror films. This new version of *Dracula* is a boring, tasteless horror film. Although it follows Bram Stoker's novel rather more closely than did Tod Browning 28 years ago, the few departures it makes are disastrous. The unforgettable opening, which was the best section of the earlier film, has been scrapped. There is no build-up of any kind, no *frisson* of anticipation, only Count Dracula's new librarian calling at the Castle as if he were delivering the peas. Transylvania looks suspiciously like Sussex; the Count (Christopher Lee) reminds me of nothing so much as a precocious head-prefect who's been up all night reading James Hadley Chase; and the three ghostly daughters ('ladies by their dress and manner') have become one un-

ghostly buxom brunette (no lady, judging by her dishabille) ... which brings me to the blood, in Eastman Colour, processed by Technicolor. Blood dripping on Dracula's coffin, trickling down his chin, streaming over Mina's nightie, you get it all over your hands and your neck and your teeth, and it's pumped into you and out of you, and no wonder the make-up man's name is Phil Leakey.[12]

End of review.

There are some opinions here with which one might agree or disagree – regarding the alleged limitations in set design and the adequacy of Lee's performance as well as what Dyer clearly sees as the general crudeness of the project. More problematic, perhaps, is Dyer's penchant for scoring points off the film. The jokes about James Hadley Chase, a British writer of American-style hardboiled thrillers, and the makeup artist's name do not really tell us anything about the film or Dyer's critical evaluation of it. Instead they speak very forcefully of Dyer's feelings of superiority to and distance from it; one suspects that he would have been altogether more respectful of the latest European art film, even if he had not liked it.

The sense that *Dracula* is a good film to make jokes about is apparent elsewhere. 'Gore blimey' exclaims one critic, while another complains that the film is too serious and needs some 'bad acting' to make it more palatable, i.e. funny.[13] Even Nina Hibbin, one of *Dracula*'s most negative critics, stated that she went to the film expecting a 'nervous giggle', but for her, as for others, what should have been a source of humour became threatening and overwhelming.[14] All of these responses seem to depend on the critics' ability (or sometimes their inability) to maintain a certain superiority to the experience offered by *Dracula* as well as their general unwillingness to engage with the film on its own terms. Either critics see the film (and the audience for which it was intended) from a safe distance or it is altogether too close for comfort and consequently becomes a dangerous and disgusting object.

Dyer's review prompted a letter from a Margery Barwick in the next issue of *Films and Filming*. As with Dyer, it is worth quoting this letter at length, partly because it is the only response to the film that I have been able to find from the late 1950s that explicitly resists the evaluative terms of reference apparent in the professional reviews but mainly because it seems to me to be one of the most balanced and perceptive reviews that the Hammer *Dracula* received. It says something about the British critical establishment that it was produced by a non-professional reviewer.

If your critic, Peter John Dyer, did not enjoy *Dracula* when he saw it, he certainly enjoyed himself later, when writing his review. So, in fact, have a large proportion of the professional critics; who, almost without exception, and charging their pens with contempt, veiled sarcasm and varying degrees of disgust, have condemned this film out of hand.

At the outset, I would say that my own first reaction to the debut of this remake was, and still is, complete revulsion to what can only be described as the bloody-minded (in more senses than one) preliminary propaganda. Have Hammer Productions frightened themselves so much, that they daren't let their work stand on its own merits? I suggest that both they and the press have done actual and quite unnecessary harm to the film and have shown a complete disregard for its good points – and it has quite a lot – simply because of this spate of gory and money-scrabbling publicity.

Don't dare see the film alone!! I have, and I am still alive to tell the tale!

We found ourselves watching what is, in fact, an exceptionally good thriller of the 'grand guignol' school, which is quite capable of holding attention without 'gimmicks'. Melodrama has, for hundreds of years, been good entertainment and sure-fire box-office. There's nothing whatever wrong with that. It admittedly employs shock tactics; but it is also so fantastic and unreal that it is, in its way, a catharsis. Never will one be tempted to suck blood, or get a 'do-it-yourself' kit and create a monster. One is purged of all such unwholesome desires. But to be effective, such fantasies must be 'played straight' as any good actor knows. I think grave injustice has been meted out to the distinguished British actors who grace this film, and who, for the most part, have grasped this cardinal rule and live up to it. I must admit, in passing, that the performance of the women is generally poor.

I contend that *Dracula* is artistically extremely well done, and a big advance on its predecessors in this field.

I implore Hammer to 'play straight' with filmgoers, for once in their lives. Let them leave their parrot-cry of 'giving the public what it wants'. We have heard it *ad nauseum*. They would be a good deal nearer the truth if they said 'We are giving the public what *we* want it to want.'[15]

As with Dyer, one might agree or disagree with some of Barwick's opinions – I personally would take issue with her dismissal of the female performances in the film – but the important change is in the overall tone of Barwick's piece. While Barwick shares the distaste of other

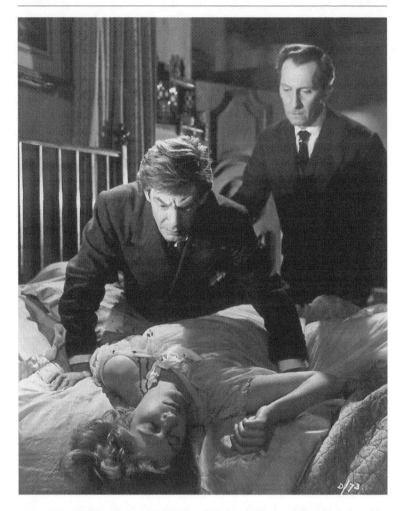

8. *Van Helsing (Peter Cushing) and Arthur Holmwood (Michael Gough) survey the aftermath of a vampiric attack on Mina (Melissa Stribling).*

critics for Hammer's marketing, she, unlike them, does not allow this to colour her reaction to the film itself. She does not make jokes and she is not appalled; instead she offers an account of *Dracula* from the perspective of an audience. The 'We found ourselves watching ...' in the fourth paragraph of her letter emphasises her identification with a collective and public response to *Dracula*, precisely the response that the professional critics found potentially so threatening. Of course, this is not the same as saying that Barwick's voice is the voice of the audience; after all, her 'review' of the film observes most of the critical conventions deployed by the other reviews. But she does not have a problem with the audience's experience of the film. By contrast, the professional critics are obviously alarmed by the idea of a mass audience enjoying something that does not fit with the critics' notion of what good entertainment for the masses should be. To a large extent, this reflects the middle-classness of the mainstream critics, and, to be more specific, what often appears to be a Herbivorous middle-classness, an old-fashioned and somewhat patronising decency deeply offended by the Carnivorous voraciousness of Hammer horror and other exploitative film fare. It seems from this that the critical responses to *Dracula* in the late 1950s were in the main ill-equipped to deal with the new type of cinema that was emerging in Britain and of which *Dracula* itself was such a vivid product.

Later and more positive critical accounts of Hammer horror have also addressed agendas that went beyond the evaluation of any single film or group of films. Take, for example, David Pirie's book *A Heritage of Horror: The English Gothic Cinema 1946–1972*, one of the most influential texts in the formation of a positive reading of Hammer. Pirie's approach to Hammer horror has three distinct elements: first, viewing it as an important aspect of an English Gothic tradition; second, discussing it as a group of films formed by specific socio-historical pressures and anxieties; and third, identifying important film-makers working within it, notably Terence Fisher, director of the Hammer *Dracula* and most of the other classic Hammer horrors. Underpinning Pirie's concern to raise the critical profile of the English horror film was a broader commitment to genre cinema, the type of cinema which in the late 1950s most critics had found either amusing or appalling. The change in attitude to this type of material that is marked by Pirie's book can be related to a cinephile approach to film that was becoming increasingly apparent in Britain from the early 1960s onwards.

Cinephilia is a difficult term to define with any precision, but basically it describes a response to cinema characterised by passion, desire and an intense, loving fascination. Cinephiles do not just like films; they love both them and the experience of cinema itself (an attitude, one suspects, that British newspaper critics of the 1950s would have found baffling). The main vehicle for the expression of cinephile attitudes in Britain in the 1960s was auteurism.[16] Now generally seen as old-fashioned and even reactionary, auteurism was in the 1950s (in France) and the 1960s (in Britain and America) provocative and controversial, representing as it did a deliberate attempt to upset established critical attitudes towards film. The key British auteurist publication was the journal *Movie*. Like its French precursor *Cahiers du Cinema*, *Movie* devoted itself mainly to Hollywood cinema and never warmed to British cinema. Indeed, one often gets a sense from 1960s cinephile/auteurist work in general that British cinema was not particularly rewarding for cinephile approaches, that it was not a cinema about which one could be passionate.

Seen in this way, Pirie's cinephile and auteurist devotion to an area of British cinema becomes all the more striking and significant. He writes positively about commercial-exploitative films that few other critics at the time took seriously. He also dared to make comparisons between the Hollywood genre cinema so beloved by other cinephiles and British film genres previously seen as imitative and inauthentic: 'It certainly seems to be arguable on commercial, historical and artistic grounds that the horror genre, as it has been developed in this country by Hammer and its rivals, remains the only staple cinematic myth which Britain can properly claim as its own, and which relates to it in the same way as the western relates to America.'[17] In short, he finds aesthetic value in films that up until the 1970s had been either a cause for concern or a cause for a good laugh. In other respects, however, *A Heritage of Horror* is a transitional work in British film criticism; its commitment to appreciating the cinematic experience itself aligns it with 1960s cinephilia but its attention to historical context also anticipates later approaches to British cinema.

Critical perspectives on British horror shifted again in the 1980s as the result of the developing academic interest in British cinema. A key publication here was *All Our Yesterdays: 90 Years of British Cinema*, edited in 1986 by Charles Barr. A number of the essays collected in this volume offered positive evaluations of the fantasy tradition in British cinema (of which Hammer horror was a significant part).[18] This often went hand-in-hand with a concern to 'deconstruct' those realistic films which earlier critics had valued so highly.[19] The imperative here was to reconceptualise an understanding of British cinema, and to bring into critical view areas of British film that had been marginalised or ignored completely in earlier critical histories of British cinema. The years since the publication of *All Our Yesterdays* have seen a substantial growth of interest in all aspects of British film, with this resulting in a proliferation of books and articles on the subject. An inevitable consequence of this increased activity has been a fragmentation so far as methodology is concerned, with different approaches co-existing.[20] However, certain elements do underpin what is otherwise disparate work, particularly a concern to relate films to the historically specific sites of their production and their reception. To a large extent, the account of the Hammer *Dracula* offered by this book has been formed in the context of this activity.

However, it also needs to be noted that Hammer horror's position in British film culture (or at least academic film culture) has become rather an odd one. It is frequently referred to in books and articles but it is not often discussed in detail and is rarely accorded the 'revisionary' accounts received by, say, the British New Wave or the films of Michael Powell. Neither has it benefited much from a recent interest in British cult cinema for here it is often figured as the rather conventional and moralistic baseline against which the more daring work of film-makers such as Michael Reeves and Pete Walker defines itself.[21] It seems from this that, so far as British cinema is concerned, Hammer horror has over the years become part of the furniture, something so reassuringly familiar that it does not require any further critical attention.[22]

The transformation of Hammer horror from something shocking into something safe happened very rapidly. Already by the early 1960s, British newspaper critics were no longer paying much attention to the procession of horrors that were emerging regularly from Hammer's Bray studio, and as if to confirm its status as an established part of British life, the company was awarded the Queen's Award for Industry in 1968. This draining away of Hammer's shock value appears to have derived mainly from over-exposure as Hammer churned out film after film based on a particular formula. As the 1960s progressed, critics were increasingly responding to the all-too-familiar Hammer brand-name and apparently not paying much attention to individual examples of the brand.[23]

This sense of people responding to Hammer horror as a particular formula is, to a certain extent, carried over into the more positive accounts of Hammer. While allotting Hammer horror an important place in British cinema, neither Pirie's *A Heritage of Horror* nor Barr's *All Our Yesterdays* discusses any Hammer horror film in sustained detail. Even Pirie's auteurist reading of Terence Fisher's work restricts itself to a discussion of Fisher's general world-view and some specific examples of his technique. This does not mean that some Hammer films are not valued more or less highly than others; but they all tend to become illustrative of a broader type in British cinema, and it is that type, rather than specific examples of it, that becomes the focus for critical activity and evaluation. Ultimately, it seems that Hammer's aggressive self-promotion and its intensive exploitation of its own successes have made it difficult for us to view any one of its films as distinctive in its own right, even a film as distinctive as the 1958 *Dracula*.

SEQUELS AND REMAKES

All the efforts of the critics to hinder *Dracula* could not stop the film from becoming a notable commercial success in both Britain and America. Given Hammer's commercial nous, as well as the propensity of the horror genre to exploit its own successes by producing cycles of films based on those successes, it was inevitable that sequels would follow, as indeed they also did for Hammer's earlier hit, *The Curse of Frankenstein*. In the case of *Dracula*, however, Hammer was initially hampered by the fact that Christopher Lee, wary of what he termed 'Vampire overdrive', declined to play the part again for seven years.[24] It is a testament to the impression Lee had made in *Dracula* that Hammer does not appear ever to have seriously considered re-casting the role for later films.[25]

What Hammer did instead in 1960 was come up with Baron Meinster, another male vampire in the aristocratic Dracula-mould, in *The Brides of Dracula*, a film in which neither Dracula nor any of his brides actually appears. As one might have expected from what was clearly an attempt to repeat the success of *Dracula*, many of the creative personnel involved in that film were reassembled – among them director Terence Fisher, cinematographer Jack Asher, and Peter Cushing as the authoritative Van Helsing (although Lee himself was absent) – for a tale that, as with *Dracula*, stressed both the physicality and the eroticism of the vampire. In their attempt to offer something that was both familiar and distinctive, the film-makers played variations on elements that had been introduced in *Dracula*. For instance, Baron Meinster, while an aristocrat like Count Dracula, is apparently a much younger figure (although David Peel, the actor in the part, was in fact older than Christopher Lee had been when he played Dracula for the first time) who still lives with his mother in Castle Meinster and who seems to have acquired the ability to transform himself into a bat, a power denied the vampire in the 1958 *Dracula*. Much more is also made in *The Brides of Dracula* of the infectiousness of the vampire bite. This is the film where Van Helsing, for the first time in vampire-film history (and, to my knowledge, for the only time) is himself bitten by a vampire and purges the infection by applying a purifying red-hot iron to the wound.

The Brides of Dracula is a beautiful-looking film. The production

values are higher than those of *Dracula*, and Jack Asher's cinemato-
graphy is, if anything, even more lustrous than it was in the earlier film.
As a narrative, however, the film is considerably less cohesive than
Dracula was, with numerous gaping holes in the plot. In large part, this
reflects a complicated pre-production history which involved several
major script rewrites in order to transform the project from the Dracula
vehicle it was once meant to be. The end result was a film that, if
viewed as a series of set-pieces depicting the various encounters between
the forces of good and evil, works very well, but which overall lacks the
focus and the organisation of the first Hammer *Dracula*.

Hammer would produce only one more vampire film before Christopher Lee's return to the role of Dracula in 1965, and that was *Kiss of
the Vampire* in 1962. As directed by the underrated Don Sharp, *Kiss
of the Vampire* was an impressive attempt to come up with a vampire
story different from *Dracula* rather than simply a variation on it. More
a mystery-thriller than Hammer's previous vampire films, and less in
thrall to the authority of the vampire hunter (here a drunken old man),
Kiss of the Vampire anticipated the anti-authoritarian attitudes that would
start to appear in Hammer horror films from the late 1960s onwards.[26]
In terms of the Hammer vampire films that preceded and followed it,
however, it was somewhat anomalous, and its significance would not
become apparent until later.

Christopher Lee finally returned as the Count in 1965 with *Dracula
– Prince of Darkness*. Directed by Terence Fisher and written by Jimmy
Sangster (under the pseudonym of John Sansom), the film replaced *The
Brides of Dracula*'s sprawling story-line with a minimal, pared-down
plot in which some English tourists stumble into Castle Dracula and
suffer the consequences. As with both *The Brides of Dracula* and *Kiss of
the Vampire*, *Dracula – Prince of Darkness* centres on travellers who are
ignorant of vampirism (as opposed to the dissimulating but knowledgeable figure of Jonathan Harker in *Dracula*), and, as with those
earlier films, this tends to put us at a distance from these unsuspecting
innocents. In the case of *Dracula – Prince of Darkness*, this leads to
some understated comedy as the English tourists ignore or explain away
increasingly sinister portents of doom.

On one level, *Dracula – Prince of Darkness* reproduces the conflict
between savant-authority figure and vampire seen in the 1958 *Dracula*,
although Van Helsing is replaced here by Father Sandor, a no-nonsense,
rifle-wielding monk who eventually despatches Dracula by causing him
to drown in the icy moat of Castle Dracula. On another level, however,

that conflict has become less central to the film than it was in *Dracula*, and this is associated with a marginalisation of the Count that becomes increasingly apparent in the sequels that follow. Aside from his brief appearance in the pre-credits sequence (which replays the ending of the original Hammer *Dracula*), Dracula does not appear in *Dracula – Prince of Darkness* until halfway through its running length, and when he does he has no lines of dialogue.[27] As with *Dracula*, his motivation, such as it is, involves 'capturing' a woman, but while the struggle over the woman in *Dracula* carried a genuine dramatic force, here it all seems rather petty, and Dracula himself turns out to be surprisingly easy to defeat. In large part, this change in Dracula's status derives from the fact that in the first film, after his initial appearance, he became a brooding offscreen presence who only occasionally erupted into visibility, while in *Dracula – Prince of Darkness*, after the long wait for his arrival, he is perhaps onscreen too much. It seems that the more explicit Hammer became as to what Dracula wanted and what Dracula did, and the more the film-makers closed down the ambiguities associated with the Count in the 1958 *Dracula*, the more banal the vampire himself became.

The interest in *Dracula – Prince of Darkness* lies elsewhere, in its portrayal of the 'normal' people, and especially Helen, the shrewish wife-turned-vampire whose destruction by Father Sandor is far more memorable than the climactic scene of Dracula's destruction. The ritual by which Dracula is resurrected is also a memorable feature. Alan, Helen's husband, is stabbed to death by Klove, Dracula's ultra-sinister manservant, and hung upside down over Dracula's coffin and his throat cut, with his blood then causing Dracula's ashes to re-form into Dracula's body. The emphasis here is on spectacle at the expense of meaning (as opposed to the spectacle of *Dracula* which does connect more meaningfully with the film's themes), and it presages the increasingly elaborate and sometimes silly methods by which Dracula would be resurrected and destroyed in later films.

The undoubted skill with which *Dracula – Prince of Darkness* is made manages to hold it together as a cohesive experience, although it becomes less interesting after Helen's destruction. None of the remaining five Hammer Dracula films – *Dracula Has Risen from the Grave* (1968), *Taste the Blood of Dracula* (1970), *The Scars of Dracula* (1970), *Dracula A. D. 1972* (1972) and *The Satanic Rites of Dracula* (1973) – exhibits that degree of cohesion, although most of them have their points of interest. For *Dracula Has Risen from the Grave*, it is the weird colour effects deployed by cinematographer-turned-director Freddie Francis and the impressively over-the-top conclusion in which Dracula is staked with a huge crucifix and cries tears of blood before turning to dust; while *Taste the Blood of Dracula* offers what for the late 1960s was a modish and what is still a quite powerful investigation of Victorian hypocrisy.[28] Unfortunately, in neither film does Dracula himself have much to do other than be resurrected and destroyed. In the case of *Taste the Blood of Dracula* in particular, one feels that his occasional scenes are merely distractions from the more interesting events going on elsewhere. It is interesting in this respect, and a further sign of Dracula's marginality, that both these films dispense entirely with the savant-authority figures who had in earlier Hammer *Dracula* films existed in a mutually defining relationship with the vampire.

The next Dracula film, *The Scars of Dracula*, returned to the Count's castle for its main setting and replayed some of the scenes first seen in the original Hammer *Dracula* – notably the one in which a female vampire-bride deceptively claims to be Dracula's prisoner. However, the film itself, which is the cheapest-looking of all the Hammer *Dracula* films, fails to provide any interesting elaborations on the established formula (aside from a not very well realised scene in which the Count effortlessly scales a castle wall) and ultimately gives the impression that the film-makers involved had simply run out of ideas about what to do with the vampire narrative. *Dracula A. D. 1972* and *The Satanic Rites of Dracula* managed to be slightly more interesting, partly because of the reappearance in them of Peter Cushing as the vampire hunter but mainly for their clumsy attempts to place Dracula in a contemporary London setting. This somewhat desperate updating of the Hammer Dracula formula can be related to broader shifts in vampire fiction taking place from the 1970s onwards, and particularly to a move towards using contemporary settings. Dan Curtis's television film *The Night Stalker* (1972), George Romero's *Martin* (1978), and, more recently, *Buffy the Vampire Slayer* and *Angel* all spring to mind as distinguished examples of this trend. However, it is worth remembering that the standard pattern for vampire films until Hammer came along was for them to be set in the present, and what we are also seeing in *Dracula A. D. 1972* and *The Satanic Rites of Dracula*, for all Hammer's modernisation, is a return to an older approach. If nothing else, it suggested that the Hammer 'episode' in the history of vampire fiction was coming to an end as the energy of the first Hammer *Dracula* finally dissipated.

The progressive inability of the Hammer film-makers to re-imagine their version of Dracula in relation to new scenarios meant that the

9. *The female vampire (Valerie Gaunt) strikes; the unfortunate victim is Jonathan Harker (John Van Eyssen).*

figure of the vampire became increasingly predictable and tiresome. Even in the contemporary settings of the final two Hammer *Dracula* films, the Count himself remained the same as he had always been. Matters were not helped by the difficulties experienced by Hammer from the late 1960s onwards in maintaining a hold on the all-important American market, with some of the company's later films not released in America at all. Budgets, which were never generous in the first place, were reduced, and the sort of production values with which Hammer had become associated were not always evident in its films from the late 1960s and early 1970s. To a large extent, this is the standard story of any cycle of films. A successful film inaugurates a series of further films which seek to capitalise upon that initial success by establishing a formula based on the first film. Eventually audiences (and perhaps film-makers as well) lose interest in the formula, the cycle concludes, and new cycles begin elsewhere.

David Pirie has identified the period from the late 1950s to the early 1970s as one which saw an unprecedented flood of vampire films from Britain, America and Europe, with Hammer a market leader for much of this time.[29] One product of the decline in the total number of vampire films from the early 1970s onwards was that there were no more substantial cycles of vampire films but instead just isolated projects with an occasional sequel. The increasing importance to the horror genre of contemporary settings also meant that the Gothic vampire stories associated with Hammer started to look decidedly old-fashioned and out-of-place.[30]

Having said this, *Dracula* adaptations were still appearing, albeit more intermittently than before. Each of them, and particularly the adaptations from the late 1960s and 1970s, sought to offer an approach to the Stoker story different from that fashioned by Hammer. In effect, they did to the Hammer version of *Dracula* what the Hammer film-makers had done to the Universal version of *Dracula* back in the late 1950s, taking something well established and familiar and introducing into it shockingly new and innovatory elements. Certain strategies emerged in respect of what was essentially a process of product differentiation. One was to recover elements from Stoker's novel that had not featured in previous adaptations.[31] So the Spanish *El Conde Dracula* (1969), directed by exploitation expert Jesus Franco and starring a moustachioed Christopher Lee as the Count, had Dracula acquiring an increasingly youthful appearance as the film progressed (an idea that *Bram Stoker's Dracula*, directed by Francis Coppola in 1993, would also deploy); while the epic BBC television version from 1977, which had Louis Jourdan as Dracula and Frank Finlay as Van Helsing, painstakingly included more elements from the novel than, probably, any other version before or since.[32] Another television adaptation of *Dracula*, this time an American version directed by Dan Curtis in 1973, proclaimed its own originality by being the first adaptation to explore the idea of the Count as a historical personage, as someone who had been allegedly based on the fifteenth-century Romanian nobleman Vlad Tepes, aka Vlad the Impaler.[33]

A key area in which the non-Hammer *Dracula*s from the 1970s distinguished themselves from the Hammer norm was through the appearance of Dracula himself. This was most obviously the case with Werner Herzog's 1979 remake of *Nosferatu*, in which Klaus Kinski re-created the animalistic vampire first seen in Murnau's 1922 version of the story. For the Curtis *Dracula*, the casting in the central role of Jack Palance, a stocky screen heavy best known for his performance as the villain in *Shane* (1953), was reminiscent of the casting of Lon Chaney Junior in the earlier *Son of Dracula*, with both of them provocative castings against what for the time was the dominant Dracula type. Other *Dracula*s, notably the BBC version and the 1979 American film directed by John Badham and featuring Frank Langella as the Count, continued the Hammer matinee idol type, although in the case of the 1979 *Dracula* taking the idea of the Count as romantic lover further than it had ever been taken before.[34]

Often underpinning this creative activity was a broader conceptual reworking of the *Dracula* narrative. Numerous historians of the horror genre have pointed out that 1970s horror cinema was less able or willing to provide the moralistic narrative closures associated with earlier types of horror cinema. The apparent failure of 'goodness' manifests itself in 1970s *Dracula* films both in the pathos often afforded the vampire himself and in a greater willingness on the part of the film-makers not to have their vampires comprehensively defeated at the end of the films in which they appear. So in Herzog's *Nosferatu*, a vampiric Jonathan Harker rides off presumably to infect the world. More spectacularly, in the 1979 *Dracula* the Count stakes Van Helsing (surely a first for *Dracula* adaptations) and, in a tantalisingly ambiguous final image, seems to escape the rays of the sun and fly off into the distance.[35]

It is easy to assume from this that the post-Hammer *Dracula* films were more daring and potentially more radical and questioning of social norms than was Hammer itself. Indeed, as already noted, Hammer's function in recent accounts of the horror genre has often been to provide a moralistic–reactionary baseline against which later forms of horror, American and European, can be defined. However, such accounts tend to forget that Hammer horror was not generally perceived as moralistic when it first appeared, and that the Hammer films themselves are in important respects more complex and ambivalent than they are sometimes made out to be. The reading of the Hammer *Dracula* offered in the previous chapter has already suggested that the film's conclusion is, in its understated way, as open as the endings of later films, and the treatment of moral authority also has a degree of ambiguity to it. It follows that the difference between the Hammer *Dracula* and later versions of *Dracula* is not an absolute difference but rather a relative one. One can go further and argue that certain features of the Hammer *Dracula* live on in subsequent versions of the vampire story. Some ideas are directly 'borrowed': a vampirised Jonathan Harker showing up in both the Dan Curtis *Dracula* and Herzog's *Nosferatu*, for example. But unsurprisingly it is Hammer's portrayal of the vampire that has proven the most influential element. The physically powerful vampire, the canine-befanged vampire, the handsome and charming vampire: they are all Hammer innovations which have a continuing influence in this particular area of horror production. It is fair to say that some of the later versions of the vampire story have exploited more daringly some of the possibilities first introduced in the 1958 *Dracula* than did Hammer's own increasingly weak sequels. The 1979 *Dracula*, for instance, is a remarkable and still underrated piece of work that provocatively confounds many of our expectations of the vampire story, although it is worth noting that this was also what the Hammer film-makers were doing back in the late 1950s.[36]

It seems from this that, so far as both the critical responses and the cinematic responses are concerned, it has become difficult to view the Hammer 1958 *Dracula* as a film in its own right. From its original release, critics have located it in relation to and seen it as a symptom of broader cultural issues and anxieties; and, as the years have passed, both critics and film-makers, in what is essentially an averaging-out process, have tended to view it simply as part of Hammer horror generally. In effect, the activity inspired by the film has made the film itself easily overlooked or taken for granted. In other words, the Hammer *Dracula* appears to have become a victim of its own considerable success.

Conclusion

This book began with a discussion of the 'shock value' of Hammer's own poster for *Dracula* and the way in which the film itself represented something startlingly new both for British cinema and the horror film. I should add that my own reproduction-copy of the poster was obtained back in 1976 in a 'Collector's Item' issue of a magazine called *Monster Mag*. The transition evident here from the vaguely scandalous effect of the poster in 1958 to its status as a cult classic and a 'collector's piece' in the mid-1970s resembles the reception history of the film itself as it has moved from being something shocking to being something acceptable, safe and even cosy.

Count Dracula has turned out to be one of the major cultural icons of the twentieth century, and already – with a starring role in the film *Dracula 2000* (UK: *Dracula 2001*) and a guest appearance in an episode of the television series *Buffy the Vampire Slayer* – it looks as if he has survived into the new millennium. The history of *Dracula* is a complicated one. It involves various groups of people working within different social and historical contexts to revise and renew the *Dracula* story, making it relevant and exciting again for whatever audience they are attempting to reach. It follows that the 1958 Hammer *Dracula* is just one significant episode in an ongoing series of developments and, as has already been noted, it is hard to explain how the film operates without reference to its place within the broader history of *Dracula* adaptation. Similarly, the Hammer *Dracula*'s critical reception requires a historical explanation. The film's initial impact on critics had more than a little to do with its innovatory character; the draining away of some of that power over the years was the result both of commercial exploitation by Hammer itself and of innovatory reactions against the Hammer approach by American and European film-makers. An account of the Hammer *Dracula* that sees it in this way underlines the fact that the history of *Dracula* generally is an economic history as much as it is a cultural one, and that each *Dracula* film exists in an exploitative relationship with other *Dracula* films.

Judgements still need to be made. We can work to understand why certain films were produced and why they were received in the ways that they were, but at the end of the day we still need to commit ourselves to an evaluative position. Is it a good film, or isn't it? I argue that the Hammer *Dracula* is a very good film indeed, one of the best of all the *Dracula* adaptations and one of the more remarkable films to emerge from British cinema in the post-war period. Its conceptualisation of the vampire is bold and imaginative, its technique is masterful, and the production generally is of the highest quality. I believe that it is one of the few British films from the 1950s that can sustain a lengthy textual exegesis of the kind offered by this book; and it is not surprising, to me at least, that it is one of the few British films to become a focus for cinephile devotion. Ultimately, of course, this evaluation represents my own personal judgement, and I am sure that others will challenge it. If nothing else, I hope that this book has brought the Hammer *Dracula* more clearly into view so that future discussions of its value and achievement can be based on a detailed awareness of the film itself rather than just seeing it merely as an example of the Hammer horror formula.

Notes

1. DRACULA LIVES!

1. It is worth noting that in 1958 the film versions of *Dracula* or *Frankenstein* would have been available to a British audience only via re-releases in the cinema. American audiences, by contrast, were by this stage able to view them via regular television screenings.

2. Incidentally, the poster reproduces the rather ambiguous gendered address of the advertising for the 1931 *Dracula*. References to 'The Terrifying Lover' suggest an appeal to romance (albeit here a decidedly perverse one) and a type of cinema that has traditionally been seen as appealing mainly to women. Similarly, the slogan 'Don't Dare See It Alone!' points to the film being a kind of date movie. 'Don't dare see it alone – see it with your boyfriend' would be the conventional reading of such a slogan, with the courageous male protecting the fearful female. It is often argued that horror films are directed mainly at a male audience, but here we have a poster which, so far as one can see, does not appear to be appealing directly to men, at least not in a straightforward way. Fear and subjection are invoked but directed at the females in the potential audience rather than the males. One wonders whether this marketing strategy points in fact to a broader cultural difficulty in representing male terror and male subjection in terms other than those of the feminine. For a fascinating discussion of the marketing of the 1931 *Dracula* and other 1930s horror films in these terms, see Berenstein, *Attack of the Leading Ladies*.

3. MacGillivray, '*Dracula*: Bram Stoker's Spoiled Masterpiece', pp. 518–27.

4. Punter, *The Literature of Terror: Volume 2*, p. 16.

5. Skal, *The Monster Show*, p. 83.

6. Jackson, *Fantasy*, p. 97.

7. See Skal, *The Monster Show*, pp. 82–3 for a brief discussion of this particular literary conspiracy theory.

8. Pope, 'Writing and Biting in *Dracula*', p. 68.

9. See Dijkstra, *Idols of Perversity*; Arata, 'The Occidental Tourist', pp. 119–44; Punter, *The Literature of Terror: Volume 2*, pp. 15–22; Moretti, 'The Dialectic of Fear', pp. 67–85.

10. Glover, *Vampires, Mummies and Liberals*, p. 9.

11. Senf, '*Dracula*: Stoker's Response to the New Woman', p. 47.

12. Dijkstra, *Idols of Perversity*, p. 341.

13. Pirie, *The Vampire Cinema*, p. 26.

14. Farson, *The Man Who Wrote Dracula*, pp. 233–5.

15. Skal, *V is for Vampire*, p. 183.

16. Ernest Jones, *On the Nightmare*, originally published in 1931; excerpt here in Frayling (ed.), *Vampyres*, p. 411.

17. Maurice Richardson, 'The Psychoanalysis of Ghost Stories', originally published in 1959; excerpt reprinted as 'The Psychoanalysis of Count Dracula' in Frayling (ed.), *Vampyres*, pp. 418–19.

18. Roth, 'Suddenly Sexual Women in Bram Stoker's *Dracula*', p. 30.

19. Dadoun, 'Fetishism in the Horror Film', p. 54. Dadoun is himself quoting Freud here on the fetish object.

20. Craft, 'Kiss Me with Those Red Lips', pp. 93–118. Craft's important article offers itself, rarely for *Dracula* criticism, as both historicist – in its reference to late-Victorian discourses on sexual identity – and psychoanalytical.

21. Twitchell, *Dreadful Pleasures*, p. 7.

22. Ibid., p. 127.

23. Ibid., p. 140.

24. Glover, *Vampires, Mummies and Liberals*, p. 2.

25. Stoker, *Dracula*, p. 457.

26. For more on Dracula as a text dealing with capitalism, see Moretti, 'The Dialectic of Fear'. 'Crew of Light' is the evocative term used by Christopher Craft in his article 'Kiss Me with Those Red Lips' to describe the young men who band together to defeat Dracula.

27. Skal, *Hollywood Gothic*, pp. 43–63.

28. Dadoun, 'Fetishism in the Horror Film', p. 55.

29. Raymond Huntley would later become a busy character actor in numerous British films, usually playing a 'bank-manager' type. According to David J. Skal, he was originally offered the title role in the American stage version of *Dracula* but turned it down because not enough money was involved (although Huntley would later tour America in the play). Given that the star of the American play, Bela Lugosi, went on to appear in the film version, there is a tantalising, never-to-be-realised possibility here that Huntley, rather than Christopher Lee, could have become the first British film Dracula. Many years later, Huntley would appear in a Hammer horror film, *The Mummy* (1959), where, in one of life's little ironies, his character was killed by the character played by Christopher Lee.

30. One might speculate that the psychoanalytical accounts of *Dracula* that identify it primarily in erotic terms are in fact seeing the novel through the filter of those popular-cultural adaptations which stress the erotic qualities of the vampire over those associated with class and racial difference.

31. Stoker, *Dracula*, p. 25.

32. Ibid., p. 28.

33. The film's sequel, *Dracula's Daughter* (1936), began in England but did culminate in a return to Transylvania.

34. A Spanish-language version of *Dracula* was produced by Universal simul-

taneously with the Lugosi version, using the same sets but a different cast. Little seen in the English-speaking world, the Spanish version has been praised by some critics as superior to the English-language one. For details, see Skal, *Hollywood Gothic*, pp. 153–77.

35. Lon Chaney, Chaney Junior's father, had been first casting choice for the role of Dracula in Browning's 1931 version of the story, but his premature death from throat cancer had opened the way for Bela Lugosi to take the role.

36. One could argue here that both *House of Frankenstein* and the later *Abbott and Costello Meet Frankenstein* – in neither of which Frankenstein actually appears – reproduce the often-made confusion of Frankenstein and his monster (the latter of which does feature in both films listed above). However, in their credits the films themselves scrupulously list the monster as 'the Monster', not as 'Frankenstein'. It seems from this that the name of Frankenstein is being used here simply as a generic type to denote a particular sort of film without any reference in it to a character name. It is interesting in this respect that Hammer's Frankenstein cycle would be much more precise in its use of the name Frankenstein.

37. For more on *Lugosi versus Universal Pictures* see Gaines, *Contested Culture*, pp. 175–207.

38. As David J. Skal has pointed out, these struggles over the copyright control of *Dracula* have in retrospect a certain irony to them, given that the novel itself had always been in the public domain in America due to a loophole in the copyright law. 'Although Stoker had been issued a copyright certificate in 1897, and his widow a renewal certificate in the 1920s, Stoker had never complied with the requirement that two copies of the work be deposited with the American copyright office.' Skal, *Hollywood Gothic*, p. 180.

39. Frayling (ed.), *Vampyres*, p. 64.

40. Skal, *Hollywood Gothic*, p. 70.

41. For a brief discussion of the horror host, see Newman (ed.), *The BFI Companion to Horror*, p. 160.

42. *Freaks* remained banned until 1963. For more on British film censorship in the 1930s, see Richards, *The Age of the Dream Palace*, pp. 89–152; and Matthews, *Censored*, pp. 67–84.

43. Quoted in Phelps, *Film Censorship*, p. 36.

44. See two chapters from Richards (ed.), *The Unknown 1930s*; James Chapman's 'Celluloid Shockers', pp. 75–98 and Jeffrey Richards's 'Tod Slaughter and the Cinema of Excess', pp. 139–60.

45. Greene, *The Pleasure-Dome*, p. 245.

46. Doherty, *Teenagers and Teenpics*.

47. In a somewhat uncanny coincidence, one of the first Lippert-Hammer films, *The Last Page* (1951), was directed by Terence Fisher, who would later direct the Hammer *Dracula*, and featured Raymond Huntley, a notable Dracula on the London stage in the 1920s.

48. According to a publicity document issued by Hammer, the company itself had also done some rudimentary market research seeking to explain the success of

The Quatermass Experiment. Questionnaires had been sent out to cinema managers asking them whether it had been the SF or horror elements in the film that audiences had found attractive. The document does not report the outcome of this exercise, but given Hammer's subsequent history, one presumes that horror won the day.

49. Doherty, *Teenagers and Teenpics*, p. 142.

50. Apparently, a problem with Milton Subotsky's original treatment of the Frankenstein story was that it had been too close to the Universal version.

2. 'I'M DRACULA'

1. *Variety*, 28 May 1958.

2. 1962 publicity handout cited in *Little Shoppe of Horrors*, May 1984, p. 22.

3. Doherty, *Teenagers and Teenpics*, p. 150.

4. *Films and Filming*, October 1958, p. 26.

5. *Films and Filming*, September 1958, p. 33.

6. For the benefit of readers unfamiliar with the terminology of camera movement, a tracking shot, or dolly shot, is one in which the whole camera moves (usually on tracks), while a panning shot, or pan, involves the camera turning on its axis.

7. For a discussion of some of the difficulties of working in small country house studios such as Bray, Hammer's base, see Porter, 'The Context of Creativity', pp. 179–207.

8. Waller, *The Living and the Undead*, p. 113.

9. Auerbach, *Our Vampires, Ourselves*, p. 120.

10. Waller, *The Living and the Undead*, p. 113.

11. Of course, another motivation for the 'excess' of the sequence is that it is also the film's credit sequence, a fact which probably gives it some licence so far as its detachment from narrative imperatives is concerned.

12. Bernard himself has stated in several interviews that he intended the Dracula theme to function in this way. Having listened to his other scores for Hammer horror films, I have found some other examples where the main theme appears to be set to the film title. However, as the only evidence I have to support this is my own perception, I point the reader in the direction of *The Hound of the Baskervilles* (1959) and *The Devil Rides Out* (1968) only tentatively.

13. I am excluding here Max Steiner's memorable music for *King Kong* (1933) because the film, despite its subsequent reputation as a horror classic, was not generally considered to be a horror film at the time of its release.

14. For a discussion of Hammer's music, see Larson, *Musique Fantastique*, pp. 145–68.

15. See Chapter One for details of this.

16. Fisher quoted in Brosnan, *The Horror People*, p. 113.

17. Fisher seems to misremember certain things about his own film. Dracula does

not take a long time to come down the stairs; on the contrary, he moves quickly. And it is unlikely that a 1950s audience would have been expecting to see fangs. Neither Lugosi nor any of the other Universal Draculas had worn them. Their introduction in Hammer's film was one of Hammer's own innovations.

18. This possibly helps to explain the curious fact of Harker not mentioning the mysterious woman to Dracula himself.

19. Interestingly, this sequence marks the end of Dracula's dialogue with the world. He does not speak again in the course of the film.

20. As in the film's opening sequence, the cellar into which Harker ventures contains two coffins, although they are positioned differently here. In the opening sequence, the woman's coffin is only briefly glimpsed in the corner of the frame; its end points at the head of Dracula's coffin which is placed at an angle of about 45 degrees to it. There is something casual about this arrangement, as if the coffins have been put there without thought. By contrast, the scene that greets Harker is much neater and in a perverse way more domesticated. The two coffins are at right angles to each other, with the woman's coffin placed submissively at the foot of Dracula's resting place.

21. This moment also introduces the notion of the vampire being allergic to sunlight, an idea that had featured only sporadically in earlier vampire fictions but which would become central to Hammer's conception of the vampire.

22. Lee, *Tall, Dark and Gruesome*, p. 201.

23. For a full listing of Cushing's television (and stage and film) credits leading up to his role in *Dracula*, see Miller, *The Peter Cushing Companion*, pp. 174–6.

24. Craft, 'Kiss Me with Those Red Lips', p. 96.

25. Interestingly, in a later Hammer vampire film, *The Brides of Dracula* (1960), a male vampire does bite Van Helsing. Here the film-makers' discomfort with some of the implications of the bite manifests itself in the awkward composition of the scene rather than with a convenient fade-to-black.

26. This strategy of replacing a weak man with a strong man is repeated even more emphatically in a later Hammer *Dracula* film, *Dracula – Prince of Darkness* (1965), in which a henpecked husband is killed and his blood used to resurrect Dracula. The vampire then vampirises the man's wife and makes her his own submissive consort.

27. Hutchings, *Hammer and Beyond*, pp. 62–5.

28. Frayn, 'Festival', pp. 307–8.

29. See, for example, Chibnall, *Making Mischief*, pp. 14–18.

30. To confuse matters further, Hammer's next vampire film, *The Brides of Dracula* (1960), is set in Transylvania, while *Dracula – Prince of Darkness* (1965), which marked Christopher Lee's return to the role of the Count, is also set more firmly in Eastern Europe than the 1958 *Dracula*.

31. Pirie, *A Heritage of Horror*, p. 84.

32. Stoker, *Dracula*, pp. 277–8.

33. The staking of Helen, a female vampire in *Dracula – Prince of Darkness* (directed by Terence Fisher in 1965), potentially offers a more sexualised version of the act. See Prawer, *Caligari's Children*, pp. 240–69, for a critique of the film

in these terms. Elsewhere I have argued that such a reading, in prioritising the figurative over the literal, does not engage sufficiently with the relation of the scene to the rest of the film and under-emphasises the fact that the scene, like the staking of Lucy scene, is as much about male weakness as it is about male authority. See Peter Hutchings, *Terence Fisher* (Manchester, 2000).

34. Apparently Terence Fisher told Melissa Stribling to convey in this scene a sense that she had just had 'one whale of a sexual night'. Quoted in *Dracula: A House That Hammer Built Special*, May 1998, p. 13.

35. Transfusion does not have the same charge here as it does in Stoker's novel where the movement of fluid from one body to another has a clear sexual implication. In Hammer's *Dracula*, transfusion is treated more clinically, more in the style of Hammer's Frankenstein.

36. This climactic pulling down of curtains to let in light is reminiscent of, and was perhaps influenced by, the conclusion of David Lean's 1946 version of *Great Expectations* in which Pip (John Mills) tears down some curtains and opens shutters in order to show Estella (Valerie Hobson) the rotting state of Miss Havisham's house.

3. THE MARK OF THE HAMMER *DRACULA*

1. *Daily Worker*, 24 May 1958.

2. *Observer*, 25 May 1958. Lejeune also wrote an equally negative review of *The Curse of Frankenstein* in which she stated: 'Without any hesitation I should rank *The Curse of Frankenstein* among the half-dozen most repulsive films I have encountered in the course of some 10,000 miles of film reviewing.' *Observer*, 5 May 1957.

3. Pirie, *A Heritage of Horror*, p. 40.

4. *Variety*, 7 May 1958; *Daily Cinema*, 19 May 1958.

5. *The Star*, 22 May 1958.

6. *Daily Sketch*, 23 May 1958.

7. *Sunday Express*, 25 January 1959.

8. Hill, 'The Face of Horror', p. 8.

9. Karloff, 'My Life as a Monster', pp. 11, 34; Grotjahn, 'Horror – Yes It Can Do You Good', p. 9.

10. For details of this, see Barker, *A Haunt of Fears*.

11. Mosley, 'The Audience is My Enemy', p. 15.

12. *Films and Filming*, July 1958, p. 28.

13. *Daily Herald*, 23 May 1959; *The Star*, 22 May 1958.

14. One also gets a sense of this in the long last sentence of Dyer's review which, despite its mock exasperation, does present the film as a dirtying and assaultive experience.

15. *Films and Filming*, August 1958, pp. 3, 35.

16. Cinephilia and auteurism are not the same thing, but it is hard to imagine any auteurist approach that does not contain some cinephile element. For an interest-

ing discussion of the under-researched subject of cinephilia, see Willemen, *Looks and Frictions*, pp. 223–57.

17. Pirie, *A Heritage of Horror*, p. 9.

18. See in particular Julian Petley's essay 'The Lost Continent', in Barr (ed.), *All Our Yesterdays*, pp. 98–119.

19. A key example of a revisionary approach to British realist film is Hill, *Sex, Class and Realism*.

20. See Ashby and Higson (eds), *British Cinema*, a recent collection of essays, for a sense of how heterogeneous this area of film studies has become.

21. On Pete Walker, an important horror-exploitation director of the 1970s, see Chibnall, *Making Mischief* and Hunt, *British Low Culture*, pp. 142–59.

22. An important aspect of this familiarity is the fact that the Hammer horror films tend to be easily available. They have received countless television screenings since the 1970s and most of them are also available on video. One might contrast this with the critical treatment of cult directors where the difficulty in getting hold of obscure films sometimes seems an essential prerequisite to cult status.

23. Reviews certainly grew shorter and more perfunctory as the 1960s progressed. For example, one review of *The Devil Rides Out* (1968), now considered by many to be one of Hammer's best films, simply noted that 'there's not much to say about *The Devil Rides Out* except that it's the latest Hammer horror release', *Guardian*, 7 June 1968. Also relevant here as a fairly typical expression of disdain for Hammer horror's formulaic nature are Carlos Clarens's comments from 1968: 'The studio contends in the face of critical dismay that practically every one of their films has done extremely well at the box office – so Hammer does not intend to change the formula, or experiment with a new one, unless public taste changes first' – Clarens, *Horror Movies*, p. 176.

24. Lee, *Tall, Dark and Gruesome*, p. 213. However, during this period Lee did play a Dracula-like vampire in the Italian comedy *Tempi Duri per i Vampiri* (1959).

25. However, when Dracula made a brief appearance in Hammer's final Gothic thriller, *The Legend of the Seven Golden Vampires* (1974), he was played by another actor, John Forbes-Robertson.

26. For more on this change in Hammer horror, see Hutchings, *Hammer and Beyond*, pp. 130–85.

27. Apparently Lee himself refused to speak the lines that had been written for him on the grounds that they were not good enough.

28. Incidentally, *Taste the Blood of Dracula* was the first Hammer film to show Dracula visiting England.

29. Pirie, *The Vampire Cinema*, p. 6.

30. Pirie suggests that one of the reason for the decline in vampire film production was the growing availability of sexually explicit films. This is a debatable point, although it is interesting that in the early 1970s Hammer produced what was in effect a mini-cycle of three films about lesbian vampires: *The Vampire Lovers* (1970) – which was based loosely on J. Sheridan LeFanu's classic Gothic tale 'Carmilla' – *Lust for a Vampire* (1971) and *Twins of Evil* (1971). All three

featured nudity and were clearly designed to emulate the 'sex-vampire' films that had been emerging from France since the late 1960s. As was the case with Hammer's other attempts to update itself in the 1970s, this innovation did not take hold at the box-office.

31. Hammer itself also did this in some of its sequels to *Dracula*. *Dracula – Prince of Darkness* contains an attenuated version of the scene in the novel where Dracula cuts open his chest and a woman drinks from the wound. (In Hammer's more decorous version, the scene is interrupted before the drinking can actually take place.) *Scars of Dracula* features – so far as I am aware, for the first time in vampire cinema – the scene in the novel where Dracula is seen crawling lizard-like up the wall of Castle Dracula.

32. Earlier television *Dracula*s had included an American production from 1956 with John Carradine as Dracula and a 1969 British version starring Denholm Elliott as the vampire.

33. Dan Curtis was also responsible for *Dark Shadows*, a TV soap-opera from the late 1960s which featured a vampire as one of its main characters, and *The Night Stalker* (1972). The latter was a hugely successful television movie in which an intrepid journalist tracked down a vampire on the loose in contemporary America. The film spawned a television series called *Kolchak – The Night Stalker*, which in turn was an influence on a later television series, *The X-Files*.

The Curtis *Dracula* was scripted by noted American horror writer Richard Matheson (who also wrote *The Night Stalker*). In the late 1950s Matheson had written a screenplay of his contemporary vampire novel *I am Legend* for Hammer. The film was never produced because of the disapproval of the British censors. If it had been made, it could well have changed the course both of Hammer horror and of the vampire film. (Two adaptations of *I am Legend* have since appeared, *The Last Man on Earth* in 1964 and *The Omega Man* in 1971. The novel has also been identified as an influence on George Romero's classic 1968 horror film *The Night of the Living Dead*.)

It is worth noting here, if only as a reminder of the creative flux out of which *Dracula* adaptations were appearing in the 1970s, that one of Hammer's unrealised projects in the 1970s was a history-based film to be called *Vlad the Impaler*.

34. An interesting feature of *Bram Stoker's Dracula* is the way that it combines the innovatory elements introduced into the Dracula story in the 1970s – Dracula as romantic lover, Dracula as historical personage. In a curious way, Coppola's film seems nostalgic for the 1970s, a decade in which Coppola himself achieved his greatest cinematic successes.

35. This sense of a world left open to infection at a film's conclusion is also apparent in other films from this period as part of a more general sense in horror of normality being overwhelmed by the monstrous – Roman Polanski's *Dance of the Vampires* (1967) and David Cronenberg's parasite-thriller *Shivers* (1976) are just two examples of this.

36. For interesting accounts of the 1979 Frank Langella *Dracula*, see Waller, *The Living and the Undead*, pp. 93–109; and Wood, *Hollywood from Vietnam to Reagan*, pp. 108–14.

Bibliography

Arata, Stephen D., 'The Occidental Tourist: *Dracula* and the Anxiety of Reverse Colonization', in Glennis Byron (ed.), *Dracula* (London, 1999).

Ashby, Justine and Andrew Higson (eds), *British Cinema: Past and Present* (London, 2000).

Auerbach, Nina, *Our Vampires, Ourselves* (Chicago and London, 1995).

Barker, Martin, *A Haunt of Fears: The Strange History of the British Horror Comics Campaign* (London, 1984).

Barr, Charles (ed.), *All Our Yesterdays: 90 Years of British Cinema* (London, 1986).

Berenstein, Rhona J., *Attack of the Leading Ladies: Gender, Sexuality and Spectatorship in Classic Horror Cinema* (New York, 1996).

Brosnan, John, *The Horror People* (London, 1976).

Byron, Glennis (ed.), *Dracula* (London, 1999).

Chibnall, Steve, *Making Mischief: The Cult Films of Pete Walker* (Guildford, 1998).

Clarens, Carlos, *Horror Movies: An Illustrated Survey* (London, 1968).

Craft, Christopher, '"Kiss Me with Those Red Lips": Gender and Inversion in Bram Stoker's *Dracula*', in Glennis Byron (ed.), *Dracula* (London, 1999).

Dadoun, Roger, 'Fetishism in the Horror Film', in James Donald (ed.), *Fantasy and the Cinema* (London, 1989).

Dijkstra, Bram, *Idols of Perversity: Fantasies of Feminine Evil in fin-de-siècle Culture* (Oxford, 1986).

Doherty, Thomas, *Teenagers and Teenpics: The Juvenilization of American Movies in the 1950s* (Boston, 1988).

Farson, Daniel, *The Man Who Wrote Dracula: A Biography of Bram Stoker* (London, 1975).

Frayling, Christopher (ed.), *Vampyres: Lord Byron to Count Dracula* (London, 1991).

Frayn, Michael, 'Festival', in Michael Sissons and Philip French (eds), *Age of Austerity: 1945–1955* (Oxford, 1986).

Gaines, Jane, *Contested Culture: The Image, the Voice, and the Law* (London, 1991).

Glover, David, *Vampires, Mummies and Liberals: Bram Stoker and the Politics of Popular Fiction* (Durham and London, 1996).

Greene, Graham, *The Pleasure-Dome: The Collected Film Criticism* (London, 1972).

Grotjahn, Martin, 'Horror – Yes It Can Do You Good', *Films and Filming*, November 1958.

Hill, Derek, 'The Face of Horror', *Sight and Sound*, Winter 1958/59.

Hill, John, *Sex, Class and Realism: British Cinema 1956–1964* (London, 1986).

Hunt, Leon, *British Low Culture: From Safari Suits to Sexploitation* (London, 1998).

Hutchings, Peter, *Hammer and Beyond: The British Horror Film* (Manchester, 1993).

Jackson, Rosemary, *Fantasy: The Literature of Subversion* (London, 1981).

Karloff, Boris, 'My Life as a Monster', *Films and Filming*, November 1957.

Larson, Randall D., *Musique Fantastique: A Survey of Film Music in the Fantastic Cinema* (Metuchen, NJ and London), 1985.

Lee, Christopher, *Tall, Dark and Gruesome* (London, 1978).

MacGillivray, Royce, '*Dracula*: Bram Stoker's Spoiled Masterpiece', *Queen's Quarterly*, Winter 1978.

Matthews, Tom Dewe, *Censored* (London, 1994).

Miller, David, *The Peter Cushing Companion* (London, 2000).

Moretti, Franco, 'The Dialectic of Fear', *New Left Review*, November–December 1982.

Mosley, Leonard, 'The Audience is My Enemy', *Films and Filming*, August 1959.

Newman, Kim (ed.), *The BFI Companion to Horror* (London, 1996).

Phelps, Guy, *Film Censorship* (London, 1975).

Pirie, David, *A Heritage of Horror: The English Gothic Cinema 1946–1972* (London, 1973).

— *The Vampire Cinema* (London, 1977).

Pope, Rebecca A., 'Writing and Biting in *Dracula*', in Glennis Byron (ed.), *Dracula* (London, 1999).

Porter, Vincent, 'The Context of Creativity: Ealing Studios and Hammer Films', in James Curran and Vincent Porter (eds), *British Cinema History* (London, 1983).

Prawer, S. S., *Caligari's Children: The Film as Tale of Terror* (Oxford, 1980).

Punter, David, *The Literature of Terror: Volume 2 – The Modern Gothic* (London, 1996).

Richards, Jeffrey, *The Age of the Dream Palace: Cinema and Society in Britain 1930–1939* (London, 1984).

— (ed.), *The Unknown 1930s: An Alternative History of the British Cinema, 1929–1939* (London, 1998).

Roth, Phyllis A., 'Suddenly Sexual Women in Bram Stoker's *Dracula*', in Glennis Byron (ed.), *Dracula* (London, 1999).

Senf, Carol A., '*Dracula*: Stoker's Response to the New Woman', *Victorian Studies*, Autumn 1982.

Skal, David J., *Hollywood Gothic: The Tangled Web of Dracula from Novel to Stage to Screen* (London, 1992).

— *The Monster Show: A Cultural History of Horror* (London, 1993).

— *V is for Vampire: The A–Z Guide to Everything Undead* (Harmondsworth, 1996).

Stoker, Bram, *Dracula* (Harmondsworth, 1993).

Twitchell, James B., *Dreadful Pleasures: An Anatomy of Modern Horror* (Oxford, 1985).

Waller, Gregory, *The Living and the Undead: From Stoker's* Dracula *to Romero's* Dawn of the Dead (Urbana and Chicago, 1986).

Willemen, Paul, *Looks and Frictions: Essays in Cultural Studies and Film Theory* (London, 1994).

Wood, Robin, *Hollywood from Vietnam to Reagan* (New York, 1986).